DIY to the
Rescue

DIY to the
Rescue

50 Home
Improvement
Projects

Karl Champley & Amy Devers

A Division of Sterling Publishing Co., Inc.
New York

T 107503

Series Editor: Dawn Cusick

Series Designer: Thom Gaines

Cover Designer: DIY Network, Stewart Pack

Page Design: Chris Bryant

Contributing Writer: Josh Garskoff

Contributing Photographer: Daniel Schwartz

Assistant Editor: Matt Paden

Production: Jackie Kerr, Matt Paden

Copy Editor: Susan Brill

10 9 8 7 6 5 4 3 2 1

First Edition

Published by Lark Books, A Division of
Sterling Publishing Co., Inc.
387 Park Avenue South, New York, N.Y. 10016

Text © 2006, Lark Books
Photography © 2006, DIY Network

Distributed in Canada by Sterling Publishing,
c/o Canadian Manda Group, 165 Dufferin Street
Toronto, Ontario, Canada M6K 3H6

Distributed in the United Kingdom by GMC Distribution Services,
Castle Place, 166 High Street, Lewes, East Sussex, England BN7 1XU

Distributed in Australia by Capricorn Link (Australia) Pty Ltd.,
P.O. Box 704, Windsor, NSW 2756 Australia

If you have questions or comments about this book, please contact:
Lark Books
67 Broadway
Asheville, NC 28801
(828) 253-0467

Manufactured in China

ISBN 13: 978-1-57990-919-2
ISBN 10: 1-57990-919-1

For information about custom editions,
special sales, premium and corporate purchases,
please contact Sterling Special Sales Department
at 800-805-5489 or specialsales@sterlingpub.com.

Contents

DIY to the Rescue

Almost everyone has a home improvement project (or multiple projects!) running through their minds. *What if I move this wall and add some windows? Suppose we replace the flooring and create some storage space? Just how difficult would it be to remove every fixture and feature in this room that reeks of a decade best forgotten?*

Ideally, moving a home improvement project from the idea stage to completion involves a fair amount of research and planning. Do you have the needed skills? The right tools? Is there a more economical approach? Occasionally, energetic homeowners tackle projects that are a bit over their heads or require a type of planning they didn't realize was necessary until they were well into the project. That's where *DIY to the Rescue* comes in. Our show visits homeowners from a wide range of geographic areas, providing help with tools, materials, guidance, technical know-how, and, sometimes the most empowering encouragement. We show homeowners how to put their can-do attitudes to work in ways that guarantee great results.

Developing a personal relationship with homeowners as we work is always a rewarding part of the show. We've met families who stopped in the middle of a home improvement project because they ran out of money or ran out of steam. Seeing their relief as we finish a project is very heart warming, to say the least. One family we worked with had been washing their kitchen dishes in a bathroom vanity sink for months because their kitchen renovation had gone awry. Another family we worked with had a special needs' child and we helped them create a cheerful, magical bedroom for him. It was amazing to see how much blood and sweat those parents were willing to put into the project.

We also take great satisfaction watching the transformation in homeowners as their confidence and skills grow during the process. Many women we work with start off a little apprehensive of power tools, and it's fun to watch them become increasingly self-assured. By the end of our time together, they're asking for power tools for their next birthday!

This book — and the *DIY to the Rescue* show it's based on — is designed to offer inspiration, planning guidance, and the detailed how-to information you will need to successfully tackle a variety of home improvement projects yourself. As you begin to plan a project, please keep the following general tips in mind.

* Check with your local municipality to find out if permits are required and which building codes apply to your project.

* Take the time to break your project down into smaller parts, itemizing the time you anticipate each step will take, as well as what tools, materials, and skills you will need.

* Follow all safety recommendations in tool and machinery manuals and in this book's how-to. Eye and ear protection, breathing masks, and gloves are always worth the effort.
* Plan well, be safe, and have fun!

Karl Champley

Amy Devers

Karl Champley & Amy Devers
Hosts of DIY Network's *DIY to the Rescue*

DIY to the Rescue

1

Kitchens

Kitchens have received a lot of decorator attention in the last 20 years, so it's not surprising that DIYers looking for a home-makeover project often want to start there. The seven projects in this chapter will guide you through some major upgrades, from installing new cabinets and replacing drywall to more easily accomplished tasks such as tiling a new backsplash. Whether you're interested in a major remodel or just a little sprucing up, beautifying your kitchen will have a big effect on your home.

COMPLIMENTS TO THE CHEF

With good intentions, Chris had promised to revamp his bachelor-pad kitchen before his wedding, when Lexi would be moving into his home. But he just didn't have the know-how to get all of the work done. So, long after the nuptials, his new wife was living with a leaky sink, permanently stained white tile countertops, dingy cabinets without doors, and old appliances that barely worked.

Before: The old cabinets no longer had their doors, which made it impossible to hide the clutter inside. During a failed attempt at renovation, Chris had removed the backsplash, leaving torn and stained wallboard in its place.

After: New cabinets, countertops, and appliances have transformed the kitchen into an organized cooking and eating space. A hand-painted tile backsplash brings color and character to the new kitchen. Right: A few of the new wall cabinets have glass doors, so Lexi can display her colorful china.

PROJECT SUMMARY

Despite Chris' numerous attempts at repairs and fix-ups, the *DIY to the Rescue* crew knew there was only one real solution to these newlyweds' problems: An entire kitchen remodel. That meant new everything, from the appliances to the countertops to the light fixtures. And it gave the Scotts a chance to learn how to do two essential projects themselves.

Installing Kitchen Cabinets. With the old cabinets and appliances removed, putting in new cabinets is a pretty straightforward process, if you understand a few essential tricks of the trade. The job is broken down into two segments, installing the wall units and installing the base units.

Tiling a Backsplash. The family decorated their own tiles at a paint-your-own-tile shop as an inexpensive way to bring unique charm to their kitchen. They also did the tile installation themselves, learning quickly from Amy's instructions.

A

You Will Need

Tape measure	Wall cabinets
Pencil	Shims
4' level	Drill/driver
Electronic stud finder	Quick-lock or C-clamps
Screwdriver set	Wood screws
3" screws	Table saw
2x4s	½" plywood

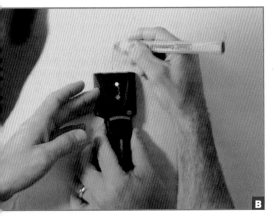

B

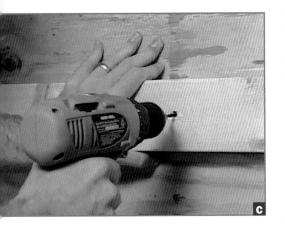

C

INSTALLING WALL CABINETS

Before the job can begin, the kitchen must be completely gutted by removing the appliances and then taking out the countertops, backsplash, and empty cabinets. In the newlywed's house, the wallboard behind the old cabinets was damaged, so the crew hung ½-inch plywood over it to even out the surface for the new cabinets and backsplash.

1 To determine the proper height for the wall cabinets, measure and make a mark 54 inches from the floor. That's where the bottom of the wall cabinets will go (to accommodate the standard 34½ inches for base cabinets, 1½-inch-thick countertop, and 18-inch-high backsplash).

2 Transfer the mark all the way around the room using a 4-foot level (photo A).

3 Use an electronic stud finder to locate all of the wall studs and mark them with a pencil. You will screw the cabinets to the studs, which will properly support their weight and will reduce the risk of an errant screw hitting plumbing or wiring inside the walls (photo B).

4 Use screws to attach a 2x4 to the wall along the level mark (photo C). Called a ledger board, this acts as a temporary support for the cabinets until they are firmly secured to the wall. Screw the ledgerboard to studs, and mark all other stud locations on the ledger with a pencil.

5 Remove all doors from the new cabinets. Place the first cabinet onto the ledger, and use the level to check its position. Place shims behind the cabinet as needed until it's plumb—perfectly vertical (photo D).

6 Follow the manufacturer's instructions for the proper location for drilling holes through the cabinet's back, and make sure that the holes align with the wall studs by referring to the marks on the ledger. Then, secure the cabinet into the studs with wood screws that are long enough to pass through the wall and go at least 1 inch into the studs.

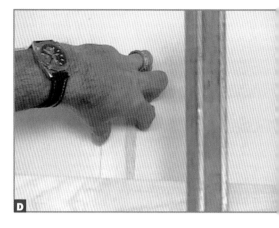

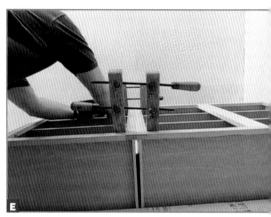

7 Lift the second wall cabinet into place, and then align and lock it into position alongside the first with quick-lock or C-clamps (photo E).

8 Predrill and countersink holes through the stiles (the vertical pieces on the face of the cabinet frames) (photo F), and insert wood screws to fasten them together.

9 Check the cabinet for plumb, then secure it to the wall studs with screws.

10 Repeat this process until all of the upper cabinets are hung. Then remove the ledger boards and attach the cabinet doors.

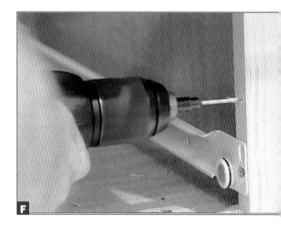

TIPS | DIY Network Home Improvement

FILLER BARS

Before installing the last cabinet in the row, hold it in place to see if there is a gap between it and the adjacent wall. If so, hide it with a filler bar, which is a matching piece of wood supplied with the cabinets. Measure the gap, and cut the bar to size on a table saw. Then, predrill holes and screw it to the side of the cabinet stile before installing the cabinet.

You Will Need

Tape Measure	Table saw
4' level	2x4s
Screwdriver set	Wood screws
3" screws	Hole saw
Electronic stud finder	Jigsaw
Drill/driver	Shims
Quick-lock or C-clamps	

INSTALLING BASE CABINETS

Base cabinets are a bit trickier to install than wall units because the floor is almost never level, so you'll have more shimming to do. Also, you'll need to work around plumbing lines for the sink and appliances.

Once the cabinets were finished, Chris and Lexi picked solid-surface countertops for their new kitchen. These are a great choice because they're extremely durable and even if they do get scratched or nicked, the damage can be sanded out. Installing solid surface countertop is not a DIY job, however. It requires an experienced installer.

1 To begin installing the base cabinets, find the floor's highest point where the cabinets will be installed. Measure up 34½ inches from that spot, and make a mark on the wall. Use a level to carry that point around the walls where the cabinets will go. That way, you can shim the cabinets up to meet the highest one as needed. (If you start at a low point, you'd have to trim the other cabinets down to that point—a much bigger job.)

2 Mark any wall studs for base cabinets that were not marked for upper cabinets, such as along a window wall for a sink cabinet.

3 Start the installation in a corner. Corner cabinets aren't able to support a countertop on their own, so first install permanent ledger boards along the mark (photo A). See the wall cabinet installation instructions for details.

4 Align the adjacent cabinet with the corner unit before fastening anything into place, because the standard cabinet will help ensure that the corner cabinet is positioned properly. Clamp the vertical stiles of the two cabinets' face frames together with C-clamps. Drill countersunk pilot holes, then fasten them together with wood screws (photo B).

5 Use the level to check the cabinets for both plumb (perfectly vertical) and level (perfectly horizontal), and use shims to make adjustments. Then, following the manufacturer's instructions, fasten them to the wall with screws driven into the wall studs that were previously marked (photo C). Repeat the procedure, adding one cabinet at a time by first attaching the stiles, then leveling, and then screwing them into the studs.

6 For the sink base, you'll need to cut holes for the plumbing lines. To do so, measure the locations of the pipes from the edge of the neighboring cabinet and up from the floor (photo D). Transfer the measurements to the back and base of the cabinet. Mark the locations for the holes, and cut them with a spade drill bit for holes less than 1½ inches and a hole saw bit for larger holes (photo E). You can also use a jigsaw. Oversize your holes a bit to allow wiggle room.

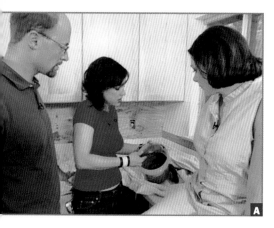

You Will Need

Measuring tape	Plastic spacers
Tiles	Scoring cutter
Mortar	Grout
Bucket	Grout float
Putty knife	Sponge
Notched trowel	

INSTALLING A TILE BACKSPLASH

Chris and Lexi decorated their own backsplash tiles at a paint-your-own-tile shop, giving their new backsplash a lot of personality. Whatever tiles you choose, here's how to install them.

1 Measure the backsplash area, and then lay the tiles on the countertop. Figure out exactly how many you need and what their arrangement will be.

2 Mix the powdered mortar with water following the proportions listed on the bag. When the mix is right, it'll have the consistency of cake frosting (photo A).

3 Beginning at one end of the backsplash, spread the mortar onto the wall using a notched trowel (photo B). Apply enough to handle a few columns of tiles—or just the first column if you're using fast-setting mortar.

4 Press the first tile into the mortar so that it's resting against the adjacent wall and the countertop (photo C).

5 Place another tile above the first, inserting two plastic spacers between them to create an even joint. Then install the next tile, with its own spacers, and so on until the first column is done. If the top tile needs to be cut to fit underneath the cabinet, use a scoring cutter to slice it.

6 Apply more mortar to the wall if needed, and begin a new column next to the first. Use spacers not only between the tiles in this column, but also between this column and the adjacent column.

7 Once the mortar has set (the set time is listed on the bag), the tiles are ready for grout.

8 Mix the grout with water, following the manufacturer's instructions.

9 Use a foam rubber grout float to apply the grout over the entire surface and to force it into the joints between the tiles (photo D). Then, remove as much excess grout as you can with the float, and use a moistened sponge to ensure that all of the joints are filled (photo E).

10 After the grout is partially dry, use a damp sponge to buff off any residue from the surface of the tile.

D

E

TIPS | DIY Network Home Improvement

SAME-DAY GROUTING

Want to grout the tiles the same day you install them? Use a quick-setting mortar. But you'll need to be careful that it doesn't harden up too quickly. Mix up and apply only small batches of mortar so it won't set before the tiles are in place.

WEEKEND UPDATE

Faced with a dark and dated kitchen, homeowners Scott and Sally weren't deterred. Scott demolished the ceiling so that an electrician could run new recessed lighting which would brighten up the work spaces. But then, he got stuck realizing that he didn't have the know-how to hang a new ceiling or complete the rest of the kitchen makeover.

Before: This homeowner needed help to hang and tape a new drywall ceiling.

After: The new ceiling looks like a professional job, and new paint and hardware have totally updated the cabinets. The kitchen also has new appliances and countertops.

PROJECT SUMMARY

The *DIY to the Rescue* crew showed Scott and Sally how to completely update and expand their kitchen without spending a lot of money. Some of the work, such as removing the wall between the kitchen and dining room, wasn't for DIYers. But Scott and Sally learned one procedure that can instantly transform any kitchen, and another that's useful throughout the entire house.

Hanging and Taping Drywall. After removing the existing ceiling to install new recessed ceiling lights, Scott needed help hanging and taping new drywall. Amy showed him the process, which can be used on any ceiling or wall throughout the house.

Painting Old Cabinets. Rather than shelling out $10,000 or more for new kitchen cabinets, Scott and Sally transformed their existing ones with new knobs and a few coats of paint.

HANGING AND TAPING DRYWALL

Scott tore down the old kitchen ceiling in order to install new recessed lighting, but he needed help putting up new drywall. Amy showed him how, and the techniques are the same for any new drywall job.

You Will Need

Drywall	Hammer and nails
Tape measure	Drywall saw
Pencil	Drywall rasp
T-square	1¼" drywall screws
Utility knife	Drill/driver
Drywall circle cutter	Chalk line

INSTALLING THE DRYWALL

1 Use 4x8' drywall, and run it perpendicular to the joists, or wall studs if you're working on a wall.

2 Starting in one corner of the room, measure from the wall to the farthest joist that your 8-foot board will reach. You need your board to end right in the middle of a joist, so find that measurement (photo A).

3 Mark the measurement on the drywall, and use a T-square to draw the line you need to cut.

4 Use a sharp utility knife to score the wallboard along that line (photo B). You don't need to press hard or get the blade deep into the board, you just need to cut the paper on the surface.

5 Give the board a push to break it along the seam (photo C), and then cut the paper on the other side using the utility knife.

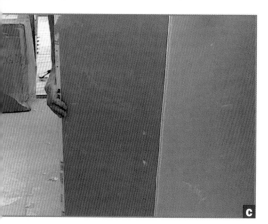

6 Measure from the two adjacent walls to the center of any light fixtures or other penetrations. Then transfer those measurements to the board. It may be helpful to lift the board into place temporarily in order to make sure you have the measurements oriented properly.

7 For cutting round openings, set the dimensions on a drywall circle cutter to match the recessed fixtures in the ceiling (photo D), and put its pin in the mark you made for the center-point of the light. Spin the tool to score the paper, then drive a nail through the board at the centerpoint (photo E). Flip the board and cut the paper from this side as well, using the hole as the center guide. Use a hammer to pop out the waste (photo F). To cut squares or rectangles, draw out the shape, get a drywall saw started by hitting it through the board with a hammer, and then use it to cut out the hole.

D

E

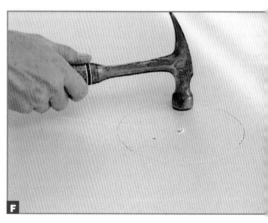

F

TIPS | DIY Network
Home Improvement

MAKING A DRYWALL TREE

A drywall tree helps to hold the board against the ceiling while you attach it. To make one, measure from the joists to the floor, subtract 2 inches and cut a 2x4 to that length. Cut another 2x4 to 3 feet. And then use 2-inch drywall screws to fasten them into a T.

8 Lift the board in place, check its fit and make any adjustments that are necessary. Shave any excess from the edges with a drywall rasp.

9 Fasten the drywall to the joists using a drill/driver and 1¼-inch drywall screws. Drive the screws far enough that they're not sticking out but not so far that they tear the paper. (They need to hold to the paper). (photo G)

10 Use five screws across each stud on each piece of drywall, making sure that each one hits wood. (Any screw that misses should be removed by backing it out with the drill/driver.)

11 Measure and cut the next board, which should butt against the edge of the first one.

12 When planning the second row, make sure to stagger the butt joints from the first row, so they'll be less noticeable (photo H).

13 Continue across the ceiling, row by row, and slice the boards in the final row to width by measuring, snapping a chalk line, and then cutting with the utility knife.

TAPING THE DRYWALL

You Will Need

6" taping knife	Sponge
Joint compound	Power sander with shop vacuum attachment and drywall dust filter (optional)
Mud tray	
Drywall tape	10" beveled taping trowel
Safety glasses	Corner trowel
Dust masks	Pencil
Fine grit sandpaper	

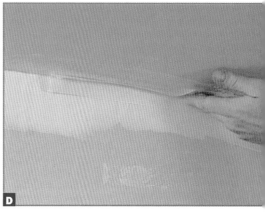

1 Use a taping knife to move some joint compound (also called "mud") into a drywall tray (photo A), so any debris that gets into the material won't contaminate the whole bucket. Leave the lid on the bucket so it won't dry out.

2 Start with the long joints, which have narrowed edges that make hiding the seams easy. Pick a joint, and use the taping knife to spread a roughly 4-inch-wide swath of mud centered over the joint (photo B). Keep it thin, no more than

⅛ inch. This essentially glues the paper tape in place.

3 Run a strip of paper tape along the seam. Use the taping knife to press it firmly and tightly against the drywall—and to squeeze any excess mud from under the tape, and remove any from the sides of the tape (photo C). Be thorough because it's much easier to remove wet mud now than to sand dry mud later. Angle your knife and "feather" it smooth to make sure not to leave a ridge at the edge of the mud.

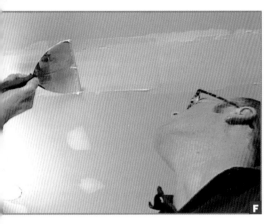

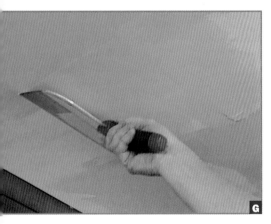

4 Repeat this process for all of the long joints. Where the ceiling meets the walls, the process is the same, except the mud goes on the wall and ceiling, and the tape is creased down the center; there's an indentation that serves as a guide for folding it (photo D, previous page).

5 Fill all of the screw heads with mud, scraping the excess material flush with the surface.

6 Let the long joints dry thoroughly (which generally means overnight) before doing the same process for the short ones, otherwise you can easily mar your completed work as you go.

7 Once the entire first coat is dry, don a dust mask and goggles, and smooth the surfaces of the mud with fine-grit sandpaper to remove any burrs or ridges. Alternatively, you can use a damp sponge, since the dried mud is water soluble. Or, you can use a power drywall sander that's attached to a Shopvac and fitted with a drywall dust filter (photo E).

8 To apply coat number two, use the taping knife to apply a roughly 6-inch-wide swath of mud over the joint (photo F), then use the knife edge to thin and smooth it so it just covers the tape, feathers

out at the sides, and has no ridges or bumps. Again, do all of the long joints first, and allow them to dry before doing the crossing joints.

9 Since the mud shrinks as it dries, repeat the process of filling all screw head indentations with mud, scraping the excess material flush with the surface.

10 Once the complete second coat is dry, then sand or sponge, and you're ready for the final coat.

11 This time apply a thin coat of mud in swaths that are 10 inches wide (photo G), and use the beveled trowel to smooth its surface and feather the edges. Use a corner trowel for areas where the ceiling meets the wall.

12 Repeat the process of filling all screw head indentations with mud, scraping the excess material flush with the surface.

13 Once the final coat is dry, give the entire surface a thorough sanding or sponging. This is the final finish, so it's a chance to sand away any bumps or ridges. Also, watch for indentations and sunken screw fills as you go. Mark them with pencil, and then come back and fill them with mud.

PAINTING CABINETS

Installing new cabinets costs many thousands of dollars—and means living without a kitchen while the work is being completed—but if you're satisfied with the layout of your kitchen, there's no need to replace your cabinets. You can modernize their style and clean up their appearance simply by painting them and replacing the knobs and pulls.

You Will Need

Screwdriver set	Paintbrushes
TSP substitute painter's detergent	Slick-surface primer
Buckets	Semi-gloss latex paint
Sponges	Paint roller
Rubber gloves	Two combination squares
Blue painter's tape	Spring punch
Two-part epoxy wood filler	Drill and drill bits
Putty knife	New hinges and knobs or pulls
Paint thinner	
Fine-grit sandpaper or sanding sponges	

1 Empty the cabinets, and then remove the doors and drawer fronts by backing out the screws. Do the same for the hinges, knobs, and pulls.

2 Wash the cabinets thoroughly with painter's detergent, which will remove grease, food residue, and the glossy sheen of the old finish. Look for a product that's labeled "TSP substitute," which means it's a similar product to tri-sodium phosphate, the traditional painters' detergent, which has largely been taken off the market. Wear rubber gloves, mix the product with water following the manufacturer's directions, and then use a sponge to wash the cabinet faces as well as the front and back of doors and drawer fronts (photo A). Wash the cabinet interiors too, if you'll be painting them.

3 Fill the old screw holes for the hardware, and any other dings and dents, using a two-part epoxy wood filler. Start by placing blue painter's tape over the back side of the screw holes (photo B) for the knobs and pulls, because they go all the way through the wood. The filler consists of an epoxy resin that you mix with a hardener before use. Mix them together on a piece of scrap wood or drywall following the manufacturer's instructions for the proportions. Don't make too much at one time because the material dries quickly once the two parts are combined (photo C).

4 Use a putty knife to press the filler into the holes, and then scrape it flush with the surface (photo D). You don't want to have to sand down big bumps later because this filler is super hard. Use paint thinner to clean the filler from your hands and tools when you're done (photo E).

5 Once the filler is dry, sand it—and the entire cabinet—with fine grit sandpaper or sanding sponges to scuff up the surfaces so that the new paint will adhere well (photo F). Remove the blue painter's tape from the back of the door.

6 Use a 3-inch brush to apply a slick-surface primer to all of the surfaces (photo G). The primer will help the paint bond to the old surfaces.

7 Once the primer is dry, give all of the surfaces a light sanding (photo H).

8 Next, apply a high-quality, semi-gloss latex paint. You can use a roller to help get paint onto the flat areas, but use the brush for edges and detailing (photo I).

9 Once the paint is dry, sand lightly again, and apply a second coat.

10 Once the second coat is dry, determine the location of the new knobs on one upper cabinet door. Then, set one combination square against the adjacent side of the door and set it to the proper depth (photo J). Set another combination square against the bottom edge to set that measurement (photo K).

11 Use the two squares to quickly locate the proper hole location on each upper door, using a spring punch to mark each hole location (photo L).

12 Repeat the process of locating the knobs or pulls for the lower cabinet doors and the drawer fronts. Then, determine placement for all hinges.

13 Use a drill bit that matches the size of the screws provided with the knobs to predrill the holes for the hardware.

14 Attach the new hardware (photo M), reattach the drawer fronts, and re-hang the doors using the new hinges.

TIPS | DIY Network Home Improvement

GLASS-FRONT CABINETS

Here's an affordable way to upgrade a few wall cabinets into a china display: Hire a glass company to cut the wood panels out of the cabinet doors and replace them with panes of glass. Options include antique, opaque, etched, leaded, or stained glass.

WALL OR NOTHING

Although homeowners Amy and Jeff had long discussed removing two walls to create an open floor plan in their home, Jeff was shocked to return from a business trip and discover that his wife had taken matters—and a sledge hammer—into her own hands and actually knocked them down. What Amy hadn't realized, however, was that one of the walls she removed was load-bearing and that removing the walls left live electrical wires dangling throughout the house.

◀ PROJECT SUMMARY ▶

Though an open floorplan made a lot of sense for this house, Amy's take-charge approach was actually quite dangerous because she could have been electrocuted, and the ceiling could have collapsed. Luckily, the *DIY to the Rescue* crew was able to make an emergency visit to the Barbles' house to show them how to fix the problems. Here's what they did.

Installing a Beam. Ideally this should be done when the wall is removed, not a few days later. It's not a do-it-yourself job—you'll need the consultation, at the very least, of a contractor or architect.

Patching a Tile Floor. A tile-patching job was required to fill in the flooring where the old walls had been.

Before: After a homeowner demolished two walls in her house, she was left with dangling electrical wires and a severe structural problem.

After: With a thick new beam hidden in the ceiling, the wiring rerouted to another wall, and a lot of drywall and trim work completed, Amy and Jeff are finally able to enjoy the results of Amy's overzealous demolition project.

Before: Removing the walls also left large gaps between the tile and oak floors in adjacent rooms.

After: With two new rows of tile and two strips of oak threshold installed, the floors show no signs that they were once separated by walls.

INSTALLING A BEAM

The reason that removing a wall isn't a DIY job is because it takes a trained eye to check whether that wall is an essential part of the home's structural support. As it turns out, one of the walls that the homeowner removed was a structural, or "load-bearing," wall, so she's lucky the attic floor didn't collapse when she removed it. But that didn't mean she had to live with the old wall. The *DIY to the Rescue* team showed her how to install a beam to carry the load that the wall once held.

You Will Need

Wood or metal bracing materials	Reciprocating saw
Safety glasses	Speed square
Gloves	Circular saw
Dust mask	½" plywood
Flat bar	Pneumatic nail gun
Hammer	3" nails
Sledge hammer	Framing nail gun
Crow bar	Joist hangers
2x12 boards	Joint compound
Two step ladders	Drywall
Tape measure and pencil	Drywall tape
Chalk line	Taping knife

1 Installing a beam requires the oversight, at least, of a contractor, engineer, or architect, who can make sure that it's properly sized and supported at each end to handle the weight that it will carry. But handy homeowners can certainly help out with the installation job.

2 Have a licensed electrician remove and reroute any wiring that's located in the wall. If there are pipes in the wall, you'll need a plumber to reroute those. These processes are best handled before the wall is removed.

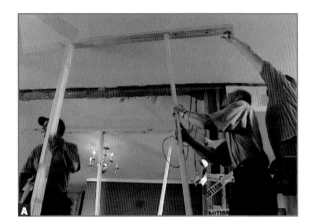

3 Build temporary bracing on either side of the bearing wall (photo A). Again, this is ideally done before the wall is removed, but in this case it happened afterward. Because this is a single story home, 2x4s were used, but for a larger building, heavier duty framing lumber or even steel bracing might be required.

4 While wearing safety glasses, gloves, and a dust mask, remove the wall by prying off all trim with a flat bar and hammer, breaking away wallboard or plaster the same way. Then, using a sledge hammer and crow bar, take out the studs and the bottom plate (being careful not to mar the floor in the process).

5 Make a simple scaffolding by laying a 2x12 across two step ladders (photo B).

6 Measure 16 inches out from either side of the former wall at each end, and snap a chalk line on each side onto the ceiling (photo C).

7 Use a reciprocating saw to cut the drywall along each line (photo D) taking care not to cut the framing inside the ceiling.

8 Use a flat bar and hammer to remove the drywall between those cuts in order to expose the ceiling framing (photo E).

9 Next, the ceiling joists need to be cut so that the new beam can slide up into the ceiling. Mark for the cuts, using the top plate as a guide (photo F), since the beam will be the same thickness.

10 Remove the top plate by prying it off the joists with a crow bar (photo G).

11 Use a speed square to transfer the marks onto the full height of the joists (photo H).

12 Cut out the joists along those marks, using a circular saw if one can fit (photo I) and a reciprocating saw if it can't.

13 To fabricate the beam for this job, the crew used two 2x12s with a piece of ½-inch plywood sandwiched in the middle (photo J). Your beam's dimensions and makeup will depend on your building. (In some cases, engineered wood or even steel I-beams are required.)

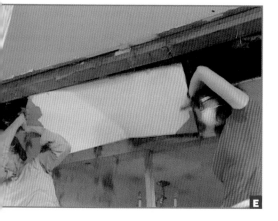

E

H

G

I

14 Look at each 2x12 from one end to determine which way they naturally bow, and align them so that they both bow in the same direction. Then mark the crown (high side) with pencil (photo K) so that it can be oriented on top of the beam to limit the chances of the beam drooping under the weight of the building.

15 Nail the beam together by sandwiching the plywood between the 2x12s, using either a hammer or a pneumatic nail gun, with four 3-inch nails every 12 inches from both sides.

16 Lift the beam into position (photo L), making sure that the crown is up and that each end is resting on a sturdy support. In this case, the existing walls at each end were beefed up with extra 2x4 studs.

17 Tack the beam in place using a framing nail gun or a hammer (photo M).

18 Install joist hangers (photo N) at every connection between the old joists and the new beam. By nailing through every prefab nail hole in these metal brackets, you're assured of super-strong joints.

19 Patch the ceiling with new drywall (photo O), joint compound, and tape (photo P). See pages 24-28 for more information about hanging and taping drywall. Remove the temporary bracing (photo Q).

PATCHING A TILE FLOOR

Removing the wall exposed a section of floor with no tile or hardwood, so some patch work was needed. This involved removing a row of existing tile that had been cut to fit against the old wall and replacing them with full-sized tiles—as well as installing a wood transition.

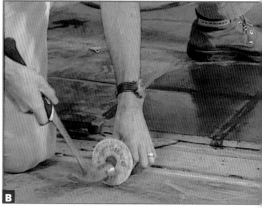

A

You Will Need

Safety glasses	Tile grout
Angle grinder	Rubber gloves
Masonry or diamond-tipped blade	Sponge float
Cold chisel	Sponge
Hammer	Wood threshold
Tile mortar	Wood stain
Notched trowel	2" finish nails
Hand trowel	Nail set
Tiles	Trim nailer (optional)
Wet saw	

B

1 Put on safety glasses before removing the old tile.

2 Load an angle grinder with a diamond tipped blade or a standard masonry blade, and use it to cut out the grout line bordering the tiles to be removed (photo A). This will help protect the rest of the floor when you're chipping out the neighboring tiles.

3 Use a cold chisel and hammer to break out the tiles that need removal (photo B) and to scrape the adhesive from the subfloor (photo C).

C

TIPS | DIY Network Home Improvement

ORDERING TILE

During any tile project, order about 10 percent more than you need. Save the extra tiles, and you'll have perfect replacement pieces in case any tiles ever chip or crack.

4 Mix concrete mortar with enough water to produce the consistency of cake frosting, meaning that it will hold peaks and valleys (photo D).

5 Use a notched trowel to spread mortar onto the subfloor (photo E).

6 Use a hand trowel to "butter" the tiles with additional mortar to account for any unevenness in the tiles, especially if they're handmade (photo F). Then lay the tiles into position on the floor.

7 Use a rented wet saw to cut tiles as needed (photo G).

8 After the mortar has cured for the time recommended on the bag, mix up a batch of grout. Use rubber gloves and a sponge float to apply the grout to the seams between the tiles (photo H). Use plenty of grout, and press it into the gaps firmly and thoroughly.

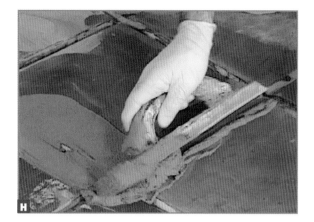

9 Wipe away the excess grout with a clean sponge and water (photo I).

10 Purchase wood thresholds (in this case oak, to match the floors in the house), and before installing them, apply wood stain to match them with the existing floor color (photo J).

11 Once the transitions are dry, cut them to fit and use 2-inch finish nails and either a trim nailer or a hammer and nail set to fasten them in place. Locate a nail every 12 inches or so, and be sure to nail into the wood only, and not into the adjacent tile (photo K).

2

Play & Work Rooms

Spare rooms are a great bonus in any home, offering a separate space for privacy, creativity, and organization. When considering a playroom or workroom remodel, there are some important questions to ask. Begin by making a list of everything you'd like to see in the room, then prioritize for time and budget. What will you use the room for most? How can you design the space for efficient workflow? What kind of light and storage do you need? With a little creativity and DIY spirit, your spare room can easily become the gem of the house.

CRAFTING A CRAFT TABLE

This family's spare room has served as everything from a baby nursery to a dog kennel. For the past several years, though, Jamie and her daughter Charlie have been using the space as a makeshift craft room. They can be found there doing everything from refinishing furniture to painting murals, creating pottery to making sculptures. And now they'd like to turn the messy, disorganized room into an efficient workspace for their projects.

BEFORE: The room was piled high with craft supplies, but it needed a complete makeover before it would be an effective craft space.

AFTER: The floors have been refinished, the walls have been painted, new cabinets hung, and a brand new custom work table has been installed.

PROJECT SUMMARY

The craft room needed everything from floor refinishing to fresh paint and new cabinets (see pages 16-19 for cabinet installation instructions). The family also wanted a large work table, which the team helped them build.

Making a Custom Work Table. Amy Devers showed the homeowners how to fabricate a custom countertop and put it on sturdy legs.

You Will Need

¾" sanded and plugged plywood	Hammer
Chalk line	Nail set
Level	Pneumatic nail gun (optional)
Tape measure	Countertop laminate
Table saw	Contact cement
Wood glue	Adhesive roller
1¼" wood screws	1" thick pine scrap
Drill/driver	J-roller
T-square	Router
Circular saw	Profiling bit
Speed square	Newel posts
1x3" inch oak trim	Wood dowels
Miter saw	L-brackets
1½" finish nails	Table cleats

MAKING THE TABLETOP

Making your own laminate countertop is less costly than buying a custom unit from a cabinet shop or home center, plus it gives you a chance to create any shape you want. For this craft table, Amy made "dog-eared" corners, which means there won't be sharp angles that could be painful to funny bones or children's heads.

1 Mark the width of your countertop at both ends of a sheet of mid-grade, ¾-inch, sanded-and-plugged plywood, which means that it has one finished surface with any knots and cracks filled and sanded smooth (photo A).

2 Snap a chalk line between the marks (photo B) and "rip" the board to size using a table saw. If the table saw is big enough, set up the rip fence to guide the wood through the blade evenly.

A

B

C

D

3 Repeat the preceding process so that you have two identical pieces of plywood the width of your countertop.

4 Arrange both boards so that their unfinished sides are up. Spread wood glue on one of them, coating the entire surface (photo C).

5 Place the other board on top of the glued surface, sandwiching the two unfinished sides together (photo D). You have two "good" sides exposed.

6 Making sure that the boards are perfectly aligned, screw them together using 1¼-inch wood screws and a drill/driver (photo E). There's no need to predrill, but make sure to sink the heads below the surface. Drive screws every 10 to 12 inches around the entire perimeter and throughout the center of the boards.

7 Next, use a tape measure and T-square to mark the length of your countertop. Set the drill/driver in reverse, and back out any screws in the area you'll be cutting.

8 Use a circular saw for this cut. In order to ensure a perfectly straight cut, it's important to set up a fence that will guide the saw. With the saw unplugged, measure the distance from the blade to the edge of the saw's base plate (photo F), and add that to the measurement you're cutting. Then use wood screws to fasten a straight scrap of wood to the plywood along that line (photo G).

E

F

G

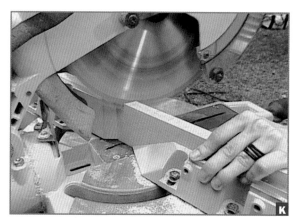

9 Now make the cut allowing the straightedge to guide the circular saw through the wood (photo H), and then remove the straightedge by backing out the screws.

10 Next, make the dog-ears on the end of the table that won't rest against a wall: Use a speed square to mark a 45-degree angle three inches from each corner (photo I), again removing any screws near the lines.

11 Cut the dog-ears with the circular saw.

12 Cut 1x3-inch oak boards to wrap around the edges of the table—except where it will butt against a wall. Measure each length (photo J), and then cut it on a miter saw (photo K). If your table has standard 90-degree angles, you'll need to make each cut 45-degrees. On this project, however, the cuts around the dog-ears needed to be 22½ degrees.

13 After checking the fit of the trim pieces (photo L), paint the inner edges of the plywood with wood glue (photo M). Then attach the oak boards so they're flush with the top of the plywood. Use 1½-inch finish nails, using a nail set to countersink the heads. Or you can use a pneumatic nail gun (photo N), which will speed up the work and greatly reduce the risk of marring the surfaces with errant hammer blows.

14 Check the surface for any high screw heads, splinters or other irregularities, and remove them.

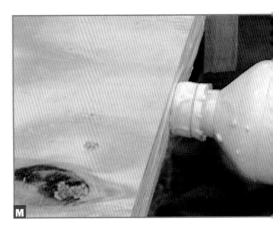

LAMINATING THE TABLE

1 Mark the tabletop's measurements onto a piece of counter-top laminate, which you can purchase at a home center or lumber yard, adding about 5 inches to the length and width. (You don't want an exact fit yet.) Cut the laminate using a circular saw.

2 To adhere the laminate to the plywood, use contact cement, which is like the industrial version of the rubber cement used for paper crafts.

3 Pour a generous amount of contact cement on both the plywood and the backside of the laminate, using an adhesive roller to spread it evenly over each surface (photo A).

4 Allow the adhesive to dry thoroughly, so that the surfaces aren't even slightly tacky.

5 Place scrap wood across the plywood every foot or so (photo B). These scraps will allow you to position the laminate over the plywood without having the two layers of contact cement touch until you're ready. (Once they make contact, you won't be able to move them).

6 Lay the laminate into position over the scrap boards (photo C), making sure that it overlaps all of the edges of the plywood and that the pattern is aligned properly with the counter-top, if necessary.

A

B

C

D

7 Starting in the middle, remove the first piece of scrap wood and, using a J-roller, gradually press the laminate into place, as a coworker removes one stick at a time, working outward from the middle (photo D). Use plenty of pressure to ensure that you remove all air bubbles.

8 Use a router to trim off the excess laminate. A profiling bit will also round the edge of the wood trim at the same time (photo E).

E

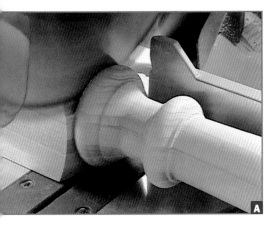

MAKING THE LEGS

1 Convert newel posts, which are sold at lumber yards for building stairway railings, into table legs by chopping off the tops (photo A) on the miter saw.

2 Cut a thin slice from one of the scrap newel post pieces, drill four evenly spaced holes in it, and use it as a template (photo B) for marking drill locations on the back of the table where each leg will go. Mark the tops of the legs too.

3 Use a ⁵⁄₁₆-inch drill bit to make ¾-inch-deep holes at each of the four marked locations on each leg and each leg location on the underside of the table.

4 Paint glue onto one end of four 1½-inch-long ⁵⁄₁₆-inch diamter wood dowels for each leg you're installing, insert them into the holes in the table, and hit their other ends gently with a hammer (photo C).

TIPS | DIY Network Home Improvement

TAPING A DRILL BIT

To take the guesswork out of drilling the holes exactly ¾-inch deep, wrap tape around your drill bit ¾-inch from the end. When the tape reaches the drilling surface, the hole is just deep enough

5 Cut a piece of 1x3-inch pine to the table's width, and fasten it to the studs in the wall at the right height for the plywood to sit (photo D). This is a cleat to fasten the table to the wall.

6 Bring the table in, put a dab of glue on the exposed end of each dowel, and attach the legs, tapping their feet with a hammer to drive them into place.

7 Stand the table on its legs, position it over the cleat, and then use L-brackets to fasten the table to the cleat (photo E).

D

E

LAUNDRY BRIGHTENER

Ami and Michael have four young children —and a lot of laundry. The laundry room was a disorganized mess. To make matters worse, the room is the first thing that the family—and guests— see when they come into the house through the garage. And the adjacent entry hall was very dark and unwelcoming since it had no windows.

Before: The laundry room had no work surfaces, poor lighting, and an ugly paint job.

After: Both the laundry room and the adjacent hallway have been brightened by the new pass-through and track lighting. And they're neatly organized too, thanks to modular storage units.

PROJECT SUMMARY

In addition to cleaning out and painting the laundry room and hall, the *DIY to the Rescue* team installed modular shelves, worktables and coat cubbies (similar to what you find at a home center, and which should be installed following the particular manufacturer's instructions). And the gang taught Ami and Michael the steps for two DIY improvement projects that can open up and brighten almost any space.

Cutting a Pass-Through. Cutting an opening in the wall between two rooms can make both spaces feel larger, brighten them by allowing light through, and provide a convenient way to transfer items from one space to the other.

Installing Track Lighting. If an existing ceiling fixture isn't bright enough, you can trade it for track lighting, which includes multiple high-wattage lamps that you can aim wherever you need the light.

You Will Need

Hammer	Drywall
Tape measure	1¼" drywall screws
4' level	Table saw
Drywall saw	Jigsaw
Utility knife	¾" birch plywood
Speed square and pencil	2" finish nails
Reciprocating saw (or handsaw)	Pneumatic nail gun or nail set
2x6s	1x6 pine boards
½" plywood	4" taping knife
2x4s	Joint compound
3" nails	Fine-grit sandpaper
2½" wood screws	Wood trim
Drill/driver	Miter saw
2" wood screws	

CUTTING A PASS-THROUGH

This project can improve a compact floor plan by making adjoining rooms feel more open. It's especially useful for old-fashioned kitchen layouts that are closed off from the eating area. A pass-through creates a more open layout and simplifies serving and cleanup.

1 Use a hammer to punch a line of holes in the wall where the pass-through will go (photo A). This will allow you to identify the stud locations and verify whether there's any electrical or plumbing lines in the way. (If there are, you'll need to bring in a professional to relocate them—or shift the position of your pass-through away from them.)

2 Measure up from the floor to mark the bottom of your opening (photo B). A good height is 40½ inches, which will make for a rough opening 42 inches high. Use a 4-foot level to mark that line.

3 Make another level line to mark the top of the new opening. Align it with the height of the nearest door or window, which means making the mark 6½ inches above the finished door opening to accommodate the framing and trim that you'll install (photo C).

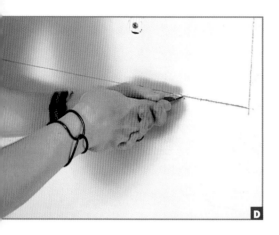

4 Use the level to mark the vertical edges of your opening, making sure that each side aligns with the inside edge of an existing wall stud.

5 Use a drywall saw and utility knife to cut the wallboard along the lines you've drawn (photo D), and remove the wallboard (photo E).

6 Now, the backside of the wallboard for the neighboring room (or in this case, hallway) is exposed. To cut it, transfer the corner locations to that wallboard using the speed square and a pencil (photo F).

7 From the open side, use the drywall saw to make the vertical cuts along each end stud—but stop the cut 5½ inches from the top (to reduce the drywall patching you'll need to do later on that side).

8 Go around to the other side and use the level to draw one pencil line connecting the tops of the two cuts and one connecting the bottoms. Then use the drywall saw to cut along those lines. Remove the drywall.

9 Use the speed square to mark the cuts to make to remove the studs at the edges of the opening. Then, use a reciprocating saw (or a handsaw) to cut the studs, being careful to make square cuts and not to damage the wallboard (photo G).

10 Now, make the "header," which will sit across the top of the opening and carry the weight of everything above it: Measure across the top of the opening from stud to stud. Then cut two pieces of 2x6 and a 5½-inch strip of ½-inch plywood to that length. Use 3-inch nails to assemble the boards so that the plywood is sandwiched between the 2x6s (photo H).

11 Next, put the end of the tape measure down into the opening below the new pass-through and measure from the bottom plate to the top of the new opening. Subtract 5½ inches, and cut two 2x4s to that length. These are the "jack studs" that will support the header at each end.

12 Position both jack studs in the wall (photo I), but press only one fully into position. Leave the other one at the ready. Then lift the header over the positioned jack stud, and bang the other one into position under it at the other side with the hammer.

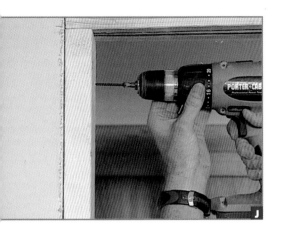

13 Use a drill/driver and 2½-inch wood screws to fasten the jack studs and header into the adjacent studs (photo J) and to each other (photo K).

14 Use 2½-inch screws to attach a piece of scrap 2x4 to each jack stud so that the tops are level with the other cut-off studs at the bottom of the opening (photo L).

15 Cut a 2x4 to fit across the bottom of the opening and screw it to the ends of the cutoff studs and scrap 2x4s using 2-inch wood screws.

16 Cut a piece of drywall (perhaps from one of the pieces you removed) to lay over the header on the side where it's exposed, and attach it using 1¼-inch drywall screws.

17 Use a table saw and a jigsaw to cut a sill from ¾-inch birch plywood. It should fit over the 2x4 and wallboard at the bottom of the opening and can extend into the room as well (photo M).

18 Attach it to the 2x4 framing using 2-inch finish nails and a pneumatic nail gun or hammer and nail set.

19 Cut 1x6 pine boards to fit snugly across the top and the two sides of the opening, and fasten them with the finish nails. (See pages 142-143 for more about cutting trim.)

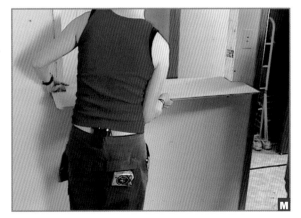

20 Use a 4-inch taping knife to apply a thin layer of joint compound to the seams around the patched wallboard (photo N), and then lay drywall tape over them and squeeze the tape flat and tightly against the wall by running the knife firmly across it. Cover the screw holes with joint compound as well.

21 When the compound is dry, sand out rough spots with fine-grit sandpaper and apply a second, thinner coat. Repeat a third time if necessary.

22 Cut wood trim to fit the opening, using 45-degree miters at the corners and finishing nails to fasten them in place (photo O).

23 Stain or paint the new woodwork.

You Will Need

Step ladder	Drywall plugs or toggle bolts
Track light	Screwdriver set
Circuit tester	Drill/driver (for toggle bolts)
Tape measure and pencil	

INSTALLING TRACK LIGHTING

The ceiling fixtures in the family's laundry room and hallway each held only one 60-watt bulb, which made the space dim and gloomy. So the *DIY* team replaced them with new track lighting, which accepts multiple high-wattage bulbs that can be aimed in any direction.

1 Throw the breaker, or remove the fuse from the electrical panel to turn off the circuit controlling the light fixture.

2 Disassemble the existing light fixture and remove it (photo A). Then, use a circuit tester to verify that there's no electricity running through the wiring.

3 Hold the new track in position on the ceiling. Use the old fixture location to center it in the room, and take measurements from the nearest parallel wall to ensure that it's positioned properly. Then, use a pencil to mark the ceiling through the mounting holes provided in the track.

4 For a lightweight fixture like this one, drywall plugs can be used to hold it in place. If your fixture is heavy, however, use toggle bolts. Drywall plugs are self-tapping, so you can just screw them into position at every mounting-screw mark (photo B). For toggle bolts, you'll have to drill holes in the drywall according to the instructions on the package.

TIPS | DIY Network
Home Improvement

WIRING SAFETY

Instead of struggling to figure out which circuit controls the light fixture, just turn off the main switch to the whole house. You'll have some clocks to reset later, but you'll save time now, and you'll be absolutely sure that there's no power running through the wiring.

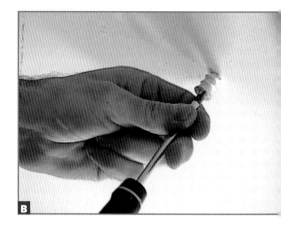

5 Hold the track in position, and use the screws provided to attach it to the drywall plugs (photo C).

6 Attach the wiring plate to the track and then make the wiring connections, following the diagram provided in the product instructions.

7 Attach the cover plate. Then attach the lighting heads to the track by inserting them and twisting them so that they lock into position (photo D).

8 Install light bulbs, turn on the power, and adjust the position of the fixtures so the light goes where you want it to.

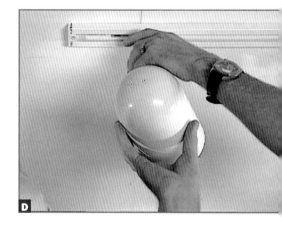

ROOM TO WORK

Trudy is a professional seamstress who works out of a makeshift sewing room that she and her husband, Ken, created in the basement. The space is dark and dank, and the poor storage and work surfaces make her back ache at the end of the day. So, Karl, Amy, and the rest of the *DIY to the Rescue* crew paid a visit to help the homeowners transform the space into an attractive and efficient workshop.

BEFORE: Trudy's sewing room lacked a large, comfortable work surface, and the old vinyl floor was bubbling and worn through in spots.

AFTER: Freshly painted walls, modular storage cabinets, new lighting, a new cork floor, and a custom sewing table have turned the gloomy basement into an efficient and eye-pleasing work area.

PROJECT SUMMARY

In addition to painting the old paneled walls, installing new light fixtures, and assembling a host of modular storage units, the team taught Trudy and Ken how to tackle two DIY projects that might help you with your own home-improvement plans.

Laying a Snap-Down Floor. These floors are durable, inexpensive, and good looking. Plus, they won't be harmed by damp basements and they're, well, a snap to install.

Building a Work Table. Here's how to make a heavy-duty work table for whatever projects you do around your home, whether they're hobbies, home improvements, or your business.

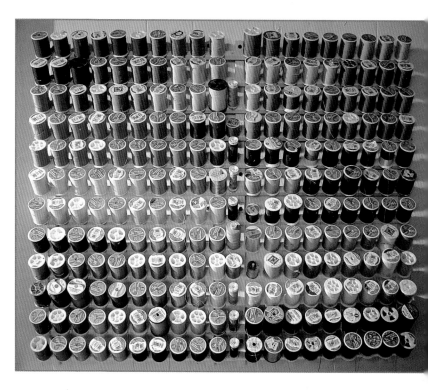

LAYING A SNAP-DOWN FLOOR

Trudy and Ken chose cork flooring for their sewing room. Made from the bark of the same Mediterranean tree used for wine corks, this flooring is comfortable underfoot and offers an attractive, natural look. Cork is also an excellent insulator, which will help to keep the basement warm. The cork planks that were used are known as snap-down flooring. They have a layer of cork on the surface with snap-together fiberboard planks underneath, and the installation process seen here can be used for any snap-down plank flooring, including faux wood, tile, and stone products.

You Will Need	
Snap-down floor planks and underlayment material	Table saw
Push broom or vacuum	Jigsaw
Wood shims	Miter saw (optional)
Tape measure	Floor pull bar (optional)
Chalk line	Thresholds
Manufacturer's tapping block	Baseboard
Hammer	

1 Prep the floor by removing the baseboard (photo A) and any old flooring that's not firmly attached, such as carpet or the loose vinyl sheeting in the Dinnhaupt's basement (photo B). Then scrape up any debris and sweep or vacuum thoroughly (photo C).

2 Bring the flooring into the room and allow it to acclimate to the temperature and humidity of the space for at least 72 hours.

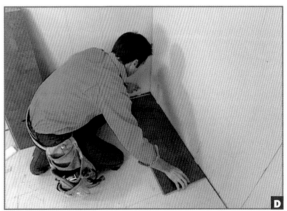

3 Lay down the underlayment sold with the flooring by following the manufacturer's instructions, which vary from one product to the next. This will act as a vapor barrier and sound-deadening material.

4 Begin in the corner adjacent to the longest wall in the room, and position a plank so that it's parallel with that wall.

5 Place wood shims, butt-end down, between the plank and the adjacent walls, in order to keep the plank ¼ inch away from the walls (photo D). This allows the floor to swell and shift with changes in humidity and heat, which it can easily do since you won't be fastening it to the floor, only to itself. Called a floating floor, this is an ideal installation for basements since changes in heat and humidity are so drastic there.

6 Repeat steps 4 and 5 at the other end of the wall (photo E).

7 Snap a chalk line between the outer edges of the two planks (photo F). You will follow this line when installing the first row of planks, ensuring that it's straight even if the wall is uneven.

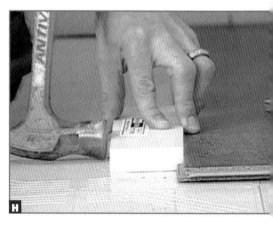

8 Working from one end (the left is ideal for right-handed workers), lay the first row of planks by placing each new plank against the first, using shims to keep it properly spaced from the wall, and making sure it rides the chalk line. Then, using the tapping block sold by the manufacturer, tap the far end of the new plank to snap it to the first plank by locking the tongue and groove joint together (photo G). You can use a scrap piece of wood instead of the tapping block, but this simple tool is shaped to mate with the board's edge, which helps to protect the board from damage (photo H).

TIPS | DIY Network
Home Improvement

DAMAGED GOODS

Inspect each plank carefully for torn edges or dented surfaces before you install it because the material can easily get damaged during shipping. Removing a damaged board later would require disassembling all of the planks installed after it.

9 Continue adding planks to the row. Where necessary, trim the wall-edge of the planks using a table saw for straight cuts or a jigsaw for notches (photo I) in order to ensure that the planks ride the chalk line and that the butt end of the shims fit between the wall and the planks.

10 You'll need to cut the last plank in the row to length. The best time to get your measurement is before you install the final, full-sized plank. That way you can shift the full plank against the spacer shims on the end, and measure the space between the two full planks (photo J) more accurately.

11 Make the cut with a table saw or large miter saw. Then, shift the full plank over, tap it into position, and install the cut piece on the end with the cut side toward the wall (photo K).

12 To stagger the rows—which hides the seams and adds strength to the floor—begin the next row with a cut plank instead of a full one (photo L), placing the cut end against the wall, as always. It's best to stagger the seams by at least 10 inches.

13 Complete the second row, and proceed row by row across the floor, using a jigsaw to cut the flooring for penetrations, such as basement poles (photo M).

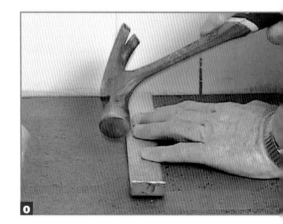

14 The final row will have to be ripped to width on the table saw. And, because you can't tap it into place, you have two options for installation. You can join it to the previous row while it's tipped at a 20- to 30-degree angle (photo N) and then drop it into position. Or, you can lay it flat and use a floor pull bar, which hooks over the outer edge and allows you to hammer it into position (photo O).

15 Lay the thresholds sold with the product over the ends of the planks in doorways, and reinstall baseboards to cover that ¼-inch gap around all of the planks (photo P).

◣ BUILDING A WORK TABLE ◢

Trudy also needed a large, sturdy sewing table where she could comfortably work without stooping. The process that Amy taught her for building her sewing table is ideal for making any work surface—from a woodworking table for the basement to a potting table for the shed to a tool table for the garage.

You Will Need

2x4s	1⅝" finish nails
Tape measure	Hammer and nailset
Circular saw	Pneumatic nail gun (optional)
Miter saw (optional)	2" foam
Drill/driver	Felt
3" screws	Scissors
2½" screws	Heavy-duty canvas
Quick-lock clamps	Staple gun
Framing square	Pneumatic staple gun (optional)
Locking casters and 3" lag bolts (optional)	Upholstery staples
¾" birch plywood	Steam iron
Combination square	Self-adhesive sewing ruler (optional)
2" screws	

1 Determine the dimensions for your tabletop and then use a circular saw or miter saw to cut two 2x4s to 12 inches less than the length (to accommodate the 6-inch overhang of the tabletop).

2 Cut 2x4s to length to fit across the table at each end and also every 16 inches across the table, subtracting 15 inches from the desired table width (to accommodate the two 6-inch overhangs as well as the two 2x4s on the ends, which each measure 1½-inches thick.)

3 Use a drill/driver to assemble the 2x4s with 3-inch screws (photo A).

4 A good sewing table height is 34 to 40 inches, but you'll want to consider the work you'll be doing at the table, as well as your own build, when deciding on the height. Subtract about ¾ inch from the finished height to accommodate the plywood tabletop (or about 3 inches if you'll be upholstering the top, and also subtract the height of the casters, if you'll be putting the table on wheels). Cut four 2x4s to that length.

5 Cut another four 2x4s to 3½ inches less than the table height.

6 Arrange the four sets of long and short boards face to face with the long boards' extra length at one end. Use 2½-inch screws to fasten them together (photo B). These are the table legs.

7 Position a leg at one corner of the tabletop, with the long board overlapping the inside edge of the long 2x4 and the short board butting against it (photo C).

8 Use a quick-lock clamp to hold the leg in place and a framing square to adjust it so it's perfectly perpendicular to the table top (photo D).

9 Secure the leg using one 2½-inch screw (photo E).

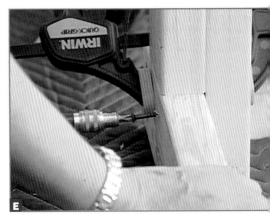

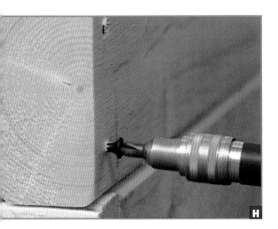

10 Remove the clamp, recheck for square, and drive in a second screw (photo F).

11 Repeat steps 7 through 10 for the other three legs.

12 Cut a 2x4 to fit across each end of the table, from outer edge to outer edge of the legs (photo G), and fasten them using 3-inch screws (photo H).

13 If you want your table on wheels, attach lockable casters to the bottom of each leg using 3-inch lag bolts sunk into predrilled holes (photo I). Flip the table onto its legs.

14 Use a circular saw with a straightedge guide (see pages 49-50, steps 8 and 9) to cut ¾-inch birch plywood for the table top. Remember to add 6 inches to the length and width of the frame for the overhang.

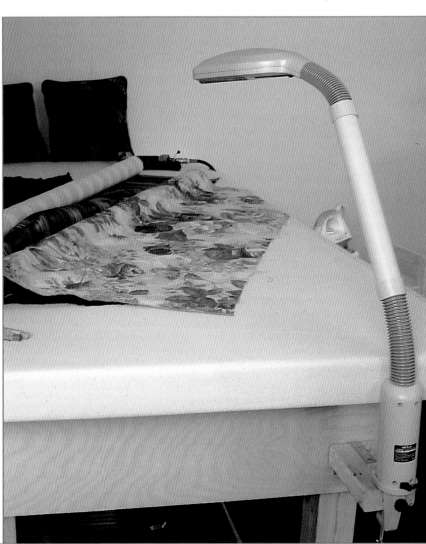

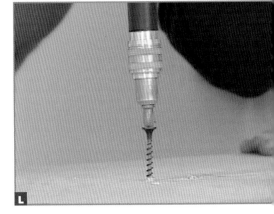

15 Orient the plywood grain to run the length of the table and, if your tabletop is larger than 4x8, plan your seam to sit on the middle of one of the 2x4 cross pieces (photo J).

16 Place the plywood on the table, set a combination square to 6 inches, and use the tool to establish the 6-inch overhang all around the table (photo K).

17 Once the tabletop is in position, secure it with 2-inch screws (photo L) around the perimeter, starting with the corners and pausing to confirm alignment between each screw.

18 Cut 6-inch strips of birch plywood as an apron to wrap around the upper portion of the legs, and fasten it using 1⅝-inch finish nails (photo M).

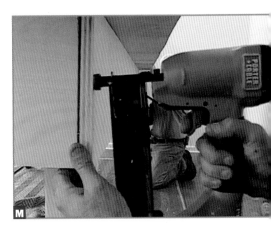

19 Cut 2x4 cross braces and fasten them across the inside edges of the legs, about 10 inches off the floor (photo N).

20 Cut a piece of plywood to create a shelf that sits on top of the cross bracing (photo O), and install it with finish nails.

21 Depending on the use of the table, you can either leave it as is, cover the plywood with Formica (see pages 52-53), or upholster it, as follows:

22 Cut 2-inch foam to the size of the top, and position it (photo P) on the table.

23 Cut a sheet of felt a few inches larger than the tabletop, and lay it over the foam (photo Q).

24 Position a sheet of canvas over the felt, and trim it to size with scissors (photo R), leaving 6 inches of extra length all the way around for tucking under the tabletop.

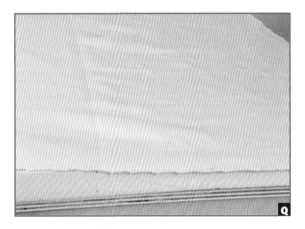

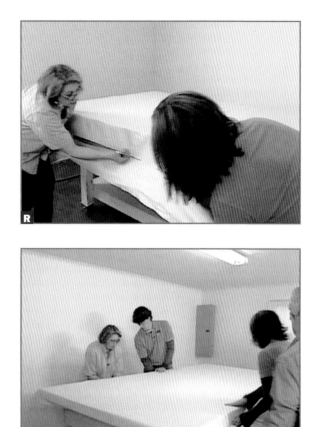

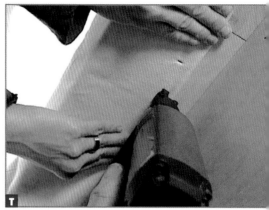

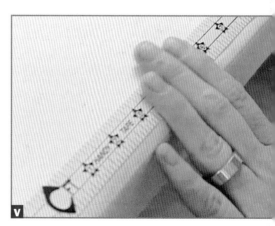

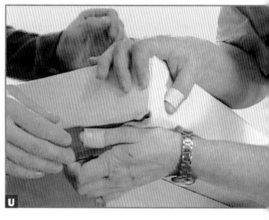

25 Stretch the canvas taut over the top (photo S), fold over the edge, and use a staple gun or pneumatic staple gun to fasten it to the underside of the tabletop with upholstery staples (photo T). Work from the center out toward the corners, starting on one long side. Then move to the opposite side, and then move from one short side to the other.

26 Save the corners for last and treat them like making a bed: Fold them into nice, tight hospital corners before stapling them (photo U).

27 Steam iron the top to shrink the fabric tight over the padding, and apply a self-adhesive sewing ruler along its edge, if desired (photo V).

FIXING A REC ROOM

David and Sandy bought a pool table as a gift for their son, Andrew, but their plans for a basement rec room never materialized. The space's unfinished ceiling, concrete floor, and raw concrete walls just weren't conducive to spending any time shooting pool. So, the table collected dust in an unused corner of the basement—until the *DIY to the Rescue* crew came on the scene, that is.

BEFORE: The basement rec room had an exposed ceiling, a bare concrete floor, and raw concrete-block walls, none of which were very conducive to spending time playing pool.

AFTER: A wood ceiling, vinyl floor, and texture-painted walls have brought color and comfort to the space.

PROJECT SUMMARY

The projects outlined in this rescue will teach you how to handle nearly any basement spruce up, whether you're planning a rec room, laundry room, media room, or children's play room.

Moving a Pool Table. One of the major problems the Anges faced with their basement remodeling plans was how to work around the pool table, which was far too heavy for them to move. The *DIY to the Rescue* team showed them how to put it on wheeled dollies and get it out of the way.

Hanging a Wood-Plank Ceiling. Wood planks offer a high-end look at a low-end price. Made from a wood veneer over a fiberboard backing, they won't lower the ceiling height the way a "drop-ceiling" would. Plus they're extremely simple to install, and they won't crack or warp from basement humidity.

Sealing Basement Walls. As hard and tough as concrete is, it absorbs water like a sponge, so dampness easily moves from the exterior of the walls to the interior of the basement. A coat of masonry sealant will close up all of the pores and prepare the walls for paint.

Laying a Sheet Vinyl Floor. A one-piece vinyl floor glues down quickly and won't be damaged by active foot traffic, basement moisture, or spilled drinks.

You Will Need

4 furniture dollies	Tape measure
Circular saw	1x6 planks
¾" plywood	

MOVING A POOL TABLE

Before the *DIY to the Rescue* crew could tackle this job, they needed to move the 2,000-pound pool table out of the way. You will need at least five people to move a heavy object like this.

1 Measure the open face of four caster-type furniture dollies. Use a circular saw to cut ¾-inch plywood to cover each dolly (photo A). Set one dolly next to each table leg.

2 Have a team of at least three people lift one side of the table, grabbing it from the base (photo B) and lifting with their legs instead of their backs, to prevent injury.

3 Meanwhile, have two other people slide a dolly under each of the two raised legs (photo C, following page).

A

B

TIPS | DIY Network
Home Improvemen

MOVING SERVICE

Don't want to move the table
yourself? Contact a local billiards
supply store to see whether they
offer a pool table moving service.

4 With a person bracing each of those dollies with a foot, repeat the process on the other side, so all four legs are on the dollies (photo D).

5 Now, wheel the pool table out of the way (photo E). Upon completion of the project, if you will maneuver over a finished floor when bringing the pool table back (such as the vinyl that will be installed in this rec room) place 1x6 runners under the wheels of the dollies to distribute the weight and protect the floors from damage (photo F)

You Will Need

- Tongue-and-groove ceiling planks with clips
- Tape measure
- Chalk line
- 1¼" finish nails
- Hammer and nailset
- Pneumatic nail gun (optional)
- Drill/driver
- 1¼" drywall screws
- Miter saw
- Drawing compass
- Utility knife
- Jigsaw
- Table saw with rip fence
- Decorative trim
- 2" finish nails

HANGING A WOOD-PLANK CEILING

These tongue-and-groove planks have a real wood surface, but it's only a thin veneer over a fiberboard backing. That's why the product is far less expensive than solid wood, much easier to install, and less prone to warping in a damp basement environment. Another big advantage is that it's extremely thin, so it will barely lower the ceiling height at all.

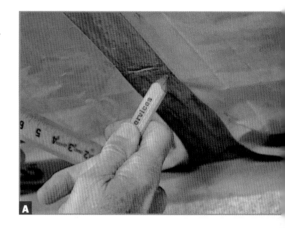

1 Make sure to store the ceiling planks in the room for at least 24 hours before installation in order to acclimate them to the temperature and humidity of the space.

2 Measure 5 inches out from each end of a wall that's perpendicular to the ceiling joists (photo A) and snap a chalk line across the joists. This is about ½ inch wider than the planks, so lining up the first row of planks with the line will ensure that they're straight and parallel with the wall, even though the planks aren't pressed tightly against the wall. The ½-inch gap will allow for expansion of the material and will be hidden by trim later. If you're using a different plank size, make your line ½ inch wider than the plank.

3 Put the first plank into position along the line. In addition to the ½-inch gap between this first row and the adjacent wall, keep a ½-inch gap between the ends of all planks and adjacent walls.

4 Fasten the plank with 1¼-inch finish nails sunk into the joists above (photo B). You can use a hammer and nailset, but a pneumatic nail gun will vastly simplify the effort of nailing overhead, and it will reduce the risk of

marring the surface with an errant hammer blow. Make sure to locate the nails near the outer edge of the plank, where they'll be covered by trim.

5 If the first plank doesn't cover the entire length of the ceiling, butt another one against it, end-to-end, and nail it in place as well. Do this as many times as necessary to complete the first row.

6 Secure the outer edges of the boards by placing one of the manufacturer's clips into the groove at every joist and fastening it in place with a screw sunk into the joist (photo C). Called blind anchors, these fasteners make the installation job simple, and you won't see them.

7 Install the next row by setting its tongue onto the clips you've already installed, and adding new clips along the plank's other side. Make sure to stagger the seams by 6 inches or more from one row to the

next, but there's no need to end the planks on a joist. The ends also have tongue and groove that will lock together and support the loose ends.

8 Cut the planks to length as necessary using a miter saw (photo D). For this job, some of the walls are angled, which necessitated some 45-degree-angle cuts, but in most cases, standard 90-degree cuts are all you'll need.

9 Repeat this process all the way across the ceiling (photo E).

10 To cut out holes for recessed lighting, make a cardboard template that's about the same size as the light cans. You can do this with a drawing compass and a utility knife.

11 Lift the board into position over the light, lay the cardboard template over the light, and mark its circumference onto the board (photo F).

12 Cut the hole using a jigsaw (photo G).

13 Rip the final row of planks to the width you need by using a table saw with a rip fence. Remember to provide for a ½-inch gap between the planks and the wall, and to face nail the outer edge close to the side so the nails will be covered with the trim.

14 Use the miter saw to cut decorative trim for the perimeter of the ceiling. You can butt square cuts together for internal corners, but use 45-degree miters for external corners, and split the total angle between each side for non-90-degree corners. (For example, the 45-degree angles in this ceiling required 22½-inch cuts on each piece of trim.)

15 Fasten the trim to the wood sill plate above the wall, if possible, by using 2-inch finish nails (photo H). If that's not possible, you'll need to use masonry screws to fasten them to the walls or perhaps to toenail them into the joists in the ceiling using finish nails.

16 Apply the face plates over the can lights (photo I), and install any hanging light fixtures, such as the new pool table light the homeowners chose.

A

SEALING BASEMENT WALLS

Paint is a great way to give basement walls some color, but moisture that moves through the concrete would eventually ruin the finish. So, Amy showed Andrew how to apply a two-part, concrete-coating system—first a sealer that will block moisture from moving through the concrete, and then a textured finish that helps to hide the outlines of the concrete block

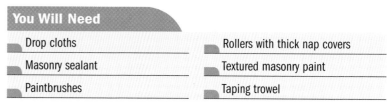

You Will Need

Drop cloths	Rollers with thick nap covers
Masonry sealant	Textured masonry paint
Paintbrushes	Taping trowel

1 Protect the floor and any furniture with drop cloths. Use a paintbrush to apply masonry sealant around the edges of the walls, and a roller with a thick nap to apply it to the rest of the walls (photo A, top left). The sealer should wick into the pores of the concrete, so that it can seal them up. If it doesn't, you'll need to work it into the surface with a stiff brush.

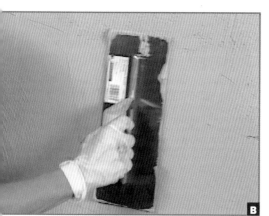

B

2 Allow the sealer to dry. Then, apply textured paint, which not only provides color but also helps to hide the lines of the concrete blocks and brings an interesting texture to the surface. It can be applied thickly or thinly. Use any number of brush strokes to produce different results. You can also apply multiple coats for a heavier texture.

3 Use a taping trowel to apply textured paint to the walls (photo B). Create the textured look you want using a stiff brush (photo C).

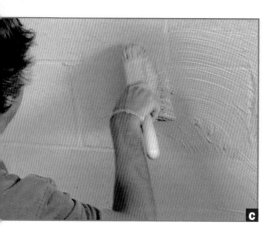

C

TIPS
DIY Network Home Improvement

CREATE A PICTURE RAIL

Want to hang pictures in your new rec room? Before painting the walls, use masonry screws to fasten a strip of 1x4 around the room (photo D). Then, paint right over it, and you'll have a rail on which to easily fasten picture hooks later.

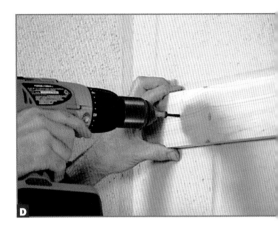

D

You Will Need

Sheet vinyl	Vinyl knife
Putty knife or wallpaper scraper	Utility knife
Broom	Vinyl adhesive
Mop	Notched trowel
Tape measure	Heavy floor roller
Paper template kit (optional)	
Scissors and vinyl – writing implement for paper template	

LAYING A SHEET-VINYL FLOOR

Vinyl flooring is extremely durable and won't be harmed by the high humidity and occasional leaks that are common in basements. And these days, you can get sheet vinyl in a host of different eye-catching designs.

1 Use a putty knife or a sharp wallpaper scraper to remove any debris that's stuck to the floor (photo A, right). Then, sweep and damp mop the floor, making sure to give the surface plenty of time to dry before you begin installing the floor.

2 For an intricately shaped floor—or if you want to be extra careful with the installation—use a paper template kit, available with the flooring. Proceed with the instructions that follow, but use the paper not the vinyl. Cut it with scissors, and then lay the resulting paper template over the vinyl, trace it, and make your cuts into the vinyl.

A

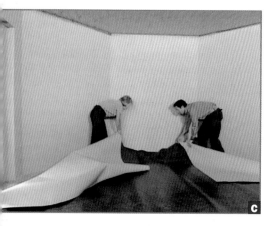

3 Roll out the sheet vinyl (photo B) and orient it properly to cover the entire space (photo C).

4 Use a vinyl-cutting knife to make a first pass at cutting the vinyl to size, leaving it oversized by a few inches around the entire perimeter (photo D).

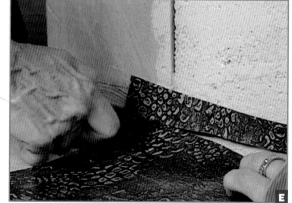

5 Make the final cut by pressing the vinyl firmly into the corners where the floor meets the walls, and slicing it using a utility knife (photo E).

6 Once the flooring is cut, carefully roll one side up and back onto the other (photo F) to apply adhesive to the floor underneath.

7 Cover every inch of the exposed floor with an even layer of vinyl adhesive using a notched trowel (photo G).

8 Allow the glue to set up for the amount of time recommended on the label, usually about 10 minutes.

9 Roll the vinyl back into position over the adhesive (photo H).

10 Roll up the other side of the sheet and repeat the gluing process for that side (photo I).

11 Run a heavy floor roller over the entire floor to press it against the adhesive and to eliminate air bubbles by chasing them to the edges of the vinyl (photo J).

OFFICE SPACE

Flower and Mark's home office gets a lot of use—it's where the couple's three kids do their homework, and it's where Flower does her college homework, too. The room's undersized desk and limited storage space were problematic, and the open floor plan between the office and master bedroom was inefficient.

◀ PROJECT SUMMARY ▶

The *DIY to the Rescue* crew did some high-level custom carpentry to build Flower and Mark a custom desk and wall shelving, as well as simple projects such as hanging new light fixtures and repainting the walls. Plus, they showed the family how to separate the office from their bedroom.

Building a Wall. Since a wall like this one has no structural weight on it, beyond supporting a door and some drywall, it's a simple DIY job.

Before: This hardworking home office was a cluttered mess—and because it opened into their master bedroom, it made their private space feel disorganized too.

After: A new custom desk and shelving, new lighting, and new paint have refreshed the room, and a new wall—complete with French doors—distinguishes the office space from the bedroom space.

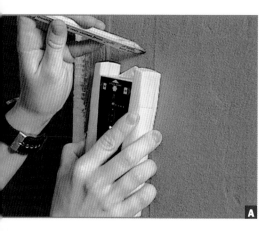

FRAMING A WALL

A home office needs to be a private room where someone can close the door and concentrate, and a master bedroom, clearly, needs privacy too. So adding this wall made a lot of sense.

You Will Need

Electronic stud finder and pencil	Hammer
Framing square	Pneumatic nail gun (optional)
2x4s	3" screws
4' level	Drill/driver
Tape measure	2½" nails
Circular saw	Handsaw
Miter saw	Drywall
Speed square	1½" drywall screws
3" nails	Prehung door

1 Use an electronic stud finder to locate the studs in the walls and the joists in the ceiling in the area for your new wall (photo A). Mark them with a pencil.

2 Use a framing square to draw a line on the floor to mark the location of the bottom plate, so it's at a 90-degree angle to the existing walls.

3 Determine the location of the door by referring to the rough opening ("RO") size listed on the door.

4 Make sure that the entire 3½-inch width of the new bottom plate can sit on the hardwood floor (photo B). If the top plate will sit only partially on hardwood, you'll need to cut back the hardwood and fasten the plate to the subfloor (see page 110, step 10).

5 Use a straight 2x4 and a level to transfer the wall location up each adjacent wall (photo C).

6 Measure the length for the bottom plate, and cut a 2x4 to that size using a circular saw or miter saw.

7 Use a speed square to mark the location where the door will go. The plate will be cut out in that spot after it's installed. Keeping it whole now helps to maintain a straight wall.

8 Use the speed square to mark the locations for studs along the plate—two at each end, another two on either side of the doorway, and single studs with their centers aligned every 16 inches elsewhere.

9 Nail the bottom plate into position with 3-inch common nails. You can use a hammer or a pneumatic framing nailer (photo D). But don't insert any nails between the marks you made for the door opening, since that material is going to be removed.

10 Cut a top plate to size and fasten it into the ceiling joists using a drill/driver and 3-inch screws (photo E).

11 The doorway will be framed as shown (photo F), with a full-size stud, then a shorter "jack" stud on each side to support a horizontal header.

12 Measure the space between the plates at each stud location, and cut 2x4s to length using a miter saw or circular saw.

TIPS | DIY Network Home Improvement

CUTTING THE DOORWAY BOTTOM PLATE

To simplify cutting out the bottom plate for the doorway, partially cut it before installation. Use a circular saw with the depth gauge set at 1 inch from the bottom side and set ¼ inch from the top side. That will make it easy to remove the remaining material later without damaging the floor.

13 Place the end studs in first and fasten them to the existing studs in the adjacent walls if possible using 3-inch nails or screws.

14 Also, "toenail" the studs into the top and bottom plates. This simply means nailing at an angle through the stud and into the plate. It's much easier to do using a pneumatic gun than a hammer (photo G). So is using a drill/driver and "toescrewing" instead.

15 Repeat this process for a companion stud adjacent to the end studs and fasten them to their partners using

2½-inch common nails and then toenail or toescrew them to the plates as well.

16 Repeat for the other studs in the wall.

17 Determine the height of the jack studs by referring to the RO size that's listed on the label for the new door.

18 Run a horizontal 2x4 header across the tops of the jack studs and short "cripple" studs between the header and the top plate, every 16 inches on center (photo H).

19 Use a handsaw to cut out the bottom plate for the door opening (photos I and J).

20 Attach drywall to the studs using 1½-inch drywall screws and a drill driver.

21 See pages 24-28 for drywalling and taping,

22 See pages 276-299 for installing and trimming out a prehung door.

TIPS | DIY Network Home Improvement

DOORWAY DRYWALL

Here's a time-saving trick for installing drywall next to a door opening (or a window opening, or the end of a wall). Overlap the drywall over the opening, and then cut it after it's attached. Use the end stud as a guide for your utility knife as you score the paper (photo at right). That saves a lot of time since there's no need to measure.

JAM SESSION

Jacque has two musicians in her household: husband Marty and son Chris. And they're both members of bands that hold practices in the basement. Because the high basement ceiling was unfinished and the floor was made of concrete, those practice sessions were deafeningly loud upstairs and didn't sound their best downstairs either, thanks to the lousy acoustics. In other words, a cool, new band practice room would definitely make all of the members of this family happy.

BEFORE: Concrete floors and an unfinished ceiling were harsh realities in the music room, making for bad acoustics and uncomfortable footing during band practices.

AFTER: A new acoustic tile ceiling, carpet tile floor, and colorful paint job have transformed the basement into a space that would make any groupie proud.

◢ PROJECT SUMMARY ◣

The crew dressed up the space with a few coats of bright green paint and a trendy carpet tile floor, for which you can see installation instructions on pages 159-162. The job also involved:

Hanging a Dropped Ceiling. Acoustic tiles have come a long way since the days of boring fiberglass rectangles punctuated with florescent lights. You can get a whole range of cool retro and modern designs that are easy to install.

Boxing in a Pipe. Here's how to hide an ugly basement pipe—or post—with an attractive wood box.

◢ HANGING A DROPPED CEILING ◣

You can buy acoustical tiles in a range of different styles that go far beyond the basic designs commonly found in commercial spaces. The sound-dampening tiles used for this project, for example, are patterned after the tin ceilings of a century ago (photo A).

You Will Need	
Acoustic tile kit	Hanger wires
Laser level	Eyelet screws
Electronic stud finder	Drill/driver
Tape measure and pencil	Eyelet screw adapter bit
Combination square	Pliers
Tin snips	Plain tiles for perimeter
Utility knife	Drawing compass
1¾" drywall screws	6"-thick fiberglass batting (optional)

1 The first step in hanging a dropped ceiling is to draw a level line around the complete circumference of the room where your ceiling will go. That's a laborious effort with a bubble level and a pencil, but it's easy with a laser level (photo B). Simply set the unit at the height you want, and it shines a row of tiny level dots on the walls. Make adjustments with the remote control, and then use the laser points for your reference line as you work.

2 Use an electronic stud finder to locate the wall studs all the way around the room, and mark their locations in pencil just above the level marks.

3 The perimeter of the ceiling grid is simply an L-shaped bracket (photo C) called a wall angle, which is designed to be installed with the short edge against the wall and the long edge supporting the ceiling tiles.

4 Use a combination square to mark 45-degree cuts on the wall angles at all corners (photo D), and make the cuts with tin snips (photo E).

B

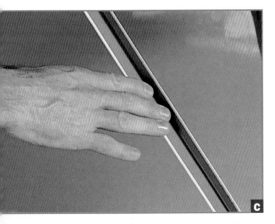

C

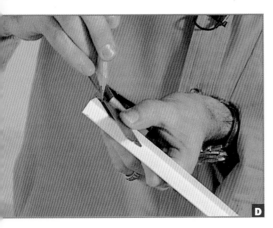

D

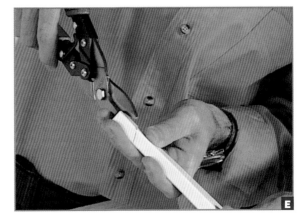

E

TIPS | DIY Network
Home Improvement

PAINTING PRIORITIES

Paint the walls before you hang the ceiling so you don't
have to "cut" the line where the walls meet the ceiling. For
this project, the crew simply painted a stripe on the wall
where the ceiling would go, so they could quickly proceed to
the ceiling installation process (photo at right) and return to
the rest of the painting later.

5 Align the bracket over the laser points (photo F) and fasten it using 1¾-inch drywall screws sunk into the wall studs (photo G).

6 The middle of the ceiling is supported by hanger wires. The standard spacing is about 4 feet between each wire, so measure and mark the locations on the bottom edges of the ceiling joists (photo H).

7 Install an eyelet screw at each location using a special adapter bit loaded into a cordless drill/driver (photo I).

8 Insert hanger wire through each eyelet screw (photo J), fold it back onto itself, and give it a few twists with pliers to hold it in place (photo K).

F

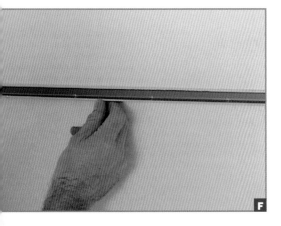

G

I

H

J

9 Measure the space between the bottom of the main support runners and their wire support holes, and adjust the laser level higher by that amount. Then, transfer that height to each hanging wire, and use pliers to create a 90-degree bend in the wires at that point.

10 Position the main support runners perpendicular to the ceiling joists every 4 feet, snap them onto the wall

angles, and slide the bent wires into their support holes (photo L), twisting the wire together a few times after the runner is in position.

11 Cut the runners and all other brackets to length with tin snips. If a piece ends in the middle of the room, simply click another piece into position next to it using the automatic latches on the ends of all runners (photo M).

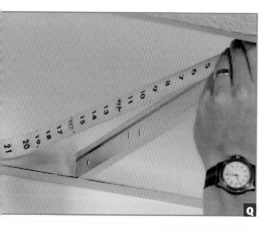

12 Fasten 4-foot cross sections every 4 feet between the main runners (photo N, previous page) and 2-foot sections every 2 feet between the 4-foot sections (photo O, previous page), snapping everything together into a grid of 2-foot squares. The patterns and procedures differ from one product to the next, so refer to your product's instructions for the exact grid-layout steps.

13 Avoid using decorative tiles around the perimeter of the room, since these tiles don't look right when they're cut. Instead, simply create a border of plain tiles around the outside edge of the ceiling.

14 Lift the tiles above the grid one by one, angling them through an opening, and then position them onto the grid from above, gently shifting the frame for alignment as necessary (photo P).

15 To trim the tiles along the edge, measure the size you need (photo Q) and cut plain tiles with a utility knife.

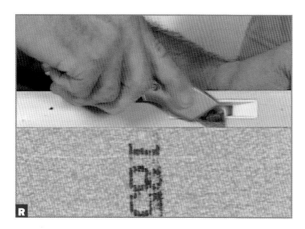

16 Re-create the reveal edge of the tile so that it will nestle into the grid properly. To do this, follow the tile's standard reveal dimensions and make a notch along the length of your cut by using a straight-edge to guide the knife into the edge of the tile (photo R) and then into the face of the tile (photo S). Remove the material in between the cuts, and lift the tile into position in the ceiling.

17 To make openings in the tile for recessed lighting that an electrician has installed, measure the diameter of the light can, and transfer it to the tile using either a compass or a cardboard template and a pencil. Then cut along the line with a utility knife (photo T).

18 For additional sound insulation, lay 6-inch thick fiberglass batting over the top of the ceiling tiles.

BOXING IN A PIPE

In this situation, an ugly pipe came down next to a wall, so the solution was a U-shaped box that was installed against the wall. But the same procedure can work for a pipe—or post—in the middle of a room as well. Just cut a fourth piece and use it to cap the U shape after it has been wrapped around the pipe.

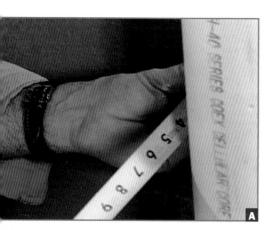

1 Measure the pipe to determine the width of the box or "chase" (photo A). Make sure to take your measurement at the widest spot on the pipe, such as a joint or a cleanout.

2 To assemble the chase, use three boards that are fastened together into a U (photo B).

3 For the two side pieces, select 1-by pine or poplar planks that are as close to the exact dimension you need as possible, but not smaller, of course. (Remember, planks are always ½-inch smaller than advertised, so a 1x4 is actually 3½ inches and a 1x8 is 7½ inches.)

4 If the plank is close to the size you need, use it as is. If it's more than a fraction of an inch wider than what you need, rip it down to size using a table saw with a rip fence.

5 The face piece will overlap the two side pieces, so you need to add their thicknesses to the width for the board. Since 1-by is actually ¾-inch thick, you'll need to add 1½ inches total to the width of the front plank. Again, either use the lumber as is, or rip it to size if necessary.

MATCHING THE PIPE CHASE

To blend the pipe chase with concrete block walls, build it to the same scale. In this case, the blocks are 16 inches long, so the face of the box was sized at 8 inches in order to make it look like it might be made from concrete block.

6 Take a measurement for the length of the box, and cut all three sides to that size using a miter saw (photo C). (For a post or pipe in the center of the room, cut a fourth plank to match the dimensions of the face piece and fasten it over the ends of the U after it has been wrapped around the post or pipe.)

7 Prime and paint the planks before installing—it's easier than painting them later. (It's a good idea to paint all of the surfaces, especially the cut ends that will sit on the floor, in order to protect them from absorbing moisture.)

8 Fasten the pieces together into a U-shape using 1½-inch wood screws sunk into predrilled and countersunk holes, making sure that the face piece overlaps the two side pieces.

9 Put the painted and assembled chase into position and screw it into the existing wall through predrilled holes, either making sure to hit the studs, or using masonry screws, in this case, for the concrete block (photo D).

3

Bedrooms

Bored with your bedroom and ready for a change? Spice things up in any number of great ways with the projects in this chapter. Try installing wall-to-wall carpeting for extra color and comfort. Or get creative by building a hip, new headboard from a vintage door. Or take a more practical approach and add a custom-built window to increase natural light. All of the projects in this chapter can help make your bedroom a more personal and intimate retreat.

QUEST FOR PRIVACY

With a toddler in arms and another baby on the way, Kathy and Tyler had to readjust their home to fit its growing population, including moving their bedroom to a former den off of the kitchen. To access this room, they used a hallway door, not the two large French doors leading into the kitchen. And those doors had become a nuisance because they limited the couple's privacy and prevented furniture from being placed along that wall—in both the kitchen and bedroom.

Before: French doors between the kitchen and master bedroom limited the furniture space in the kitchen.

After: With the old door gone, a new table and chairs have provided the family with an eat-in kitchen area.

PROJECT SUMMARY

There's no reason to live with an unwanted doorway. Walling it up is a simple job—certainly much easier than cutting a new doorway into a wall.

Eliminating a Doorway. Because there's no structural, electrical, or plumbing work involved, this is a classic DIY project. If you have some basic carpentry and drywall abilities, you can tackle it yourself.

Before: The old doors limited the furniture arrangement options in the bedroom too.

After: With the wall closed up, and some new sconces installed by an electrician, the bed has now been switched to the other side of the room, creating a far better layout.

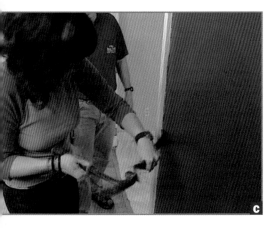

◗ ELIMINATING A DOORWAY ◗

The builder who planned your house may not have foreseen the way you would actually use the rooms, so extra doorways may impede your privacy and limit your layout options. Luckily, removing unwanted doors and walling up the openings is a straightforward job.

You Will Need

Screwdriver set	Speed square
Drill/driver	2" nails or screws
Utility knife	4' level
Flat bar	T-square
Hammer	1¼" drywall screws
Reciprocating saw	Drywall
Broom/vacuum	1¾" nails or screws
Chalk line	Fiberglass mesh drywall tape
Tape measure and pencil	Joint compound
Circular saw	Taping knife
Miter saw	Car-window squeegee
2x4s	Spray bottle with water
Pressure treated 2x4 (optional)	Baseboard trim
Masonry screws (optional)	Paint and paintbrushes
Masonry bit (optional)	Putty
3" nails or screws	Painter's caulk
Pneumatic nail gun	

1 Remove the doors by backing out the hinge screws from the door jamb (photo A).

2 Use a utility knife to score the paint around the edges of all trim (photo B). This will protect the walls from damage when you remove the trim.

3 Using a flat bar and hammer, remove the trim from the doorway on both sides (photo C). Be careful not to damage the walls.

4 Next, remove the two side jambs and then the top jamb, again using the flat bar and hammer to pry them free

(photo D). If necessary, slide through the jambs with a reciprocating saw to help free them.

5 A strip of flooring must be removed so that a 2x4, called a bottom plate, can be fastened to the subfloor underneath. In this case, the wood threshold was installed with screws, which meant digging out the putty over the heads with a utility knife and then using the drill/driver to back out the screws (photo E). For a nailed threshold, simply use a flat bar and hammer to pry it up (photo F).

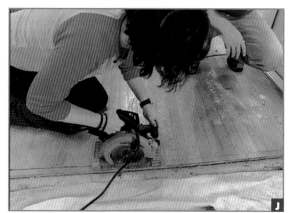

6 Snap a chalk line from the edge of the wall studs on either side of the opening to establish the line you'll need to cut across the flooring that's in the way (photo G).

7 Measure the depth of the flooring (photo H) and set the circular saw depth guide to that precise measurement (photo I) to ensure that you don't cut any deeper.

8 Cut the floorboards with the circular saw, following the chalk line (photo J). Use a reciprocating saw to get the flooring that's close to the ends of the doorway, where the circular saw can't reach (photo K).

9 Sweep or vacuum the area, take a measurement for the bottom plate (photo L), and then cut a 2x4 to that size with a circular saw or miter saw.

10 This Florida home has a concrete subfloor, so the team used pressure-treated lumber for the bottom plate, and fastened it with masonry screws by predrilling holes through the plate and into the concrete with a masonry bit (photo M). They drove the blue masonry screws into those holes (photo N). For a wood subfloor, a standard 2x4 can be nailed or screwed in place without predrilling or using specialty fasteners.

TIPS | DIY Network
Home Improvement

KEEP YOUR HARDWARE

Don't throw away old doors. Those doors, and their hardware, match what's in your house. They will come in handy in case you ever need to replace a door or a broken knob—or decide to add a new doorway, for that matter.

11 Take a measurement across the top of the opening for a top plate (photo O), which will provide good solid nailing for the new drywall.

12 Cut a 2x4 to that size and use 3-inch nails to fasten it to the existing framing above the opening. Using a hammer would be difficult for this overhead job, so use a pneumatic nail gun, or use 3-inch screws and a drill/driver.

13 Measure the height of the opening at one side, cut a 2x4 to length, and nail or screw it in place against the existing framing (photo P).

14 Repeat for the other side of the opening.

15 Place the end of the tape measure against one of your new studs, and lay it across the bottom plate. Make a mark every 16 inches (these locations—16, 32, 48—are highlighted on the tape measure). Then use a speed square to establish lines at those marks and draw an X on the side of the line where the stud should go (to the right, if the end of your tape measure was against a stud on the right of the opening, and vice versa).

16 Measure and then use a circular saw or miter saw to cut studs for each mark.

17 Using 2-inch nails, "toe-nail" them into place against the top and bottom plates, using a 4-foot level to check them for plumb left to right and front to back. Toenailing means angling the nail through the end of the stud and into the plate (photo Q). Toenailing is tricky with a hammer, but fairly simple with a nail gun. Toescrewing is also an easy alternative using a drill/driver.

18 Take a measurement from side to side in the opening, and transfer it to a piece of drywall. Use a T-square to establish the cut line, and score the drywall paper with a sharp utility knife. Holding a straightedge on the line will help guide your blade (photo R).

19 Snap the drywall along the score line (photo S), and then cut the remaining paper on the other side using the utility knife.

20 Position the piece into the opening , and use 1¼-inch drywall screws to fasten it to the new framing (photo T). Space screws about 8 inches apart along each stud—and along the new top plate—and make sure to set the heads below the surface without breaking through the paper.

21 Measure and cut additional pieces of drywall as needed to fill both sides of the framed opening. Use the largest pieces possible so that you have as few seams as possible.

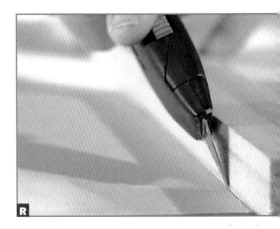

22 To tape the seams, follow the instructions on pages 27-28—or the shortcut from Karl that follows.

23 Fasten fiberglass mesh drywall tape over all of the seams by smoothing it in place with a taping knife (photo U). It's self-adhesive, but you can use adhesive spray to help it stick to the existing wall if necessary (photo V).

24 Use the taping knife to apply a generous amount of joint compound (or "mud") over the seams and screw holes (photo W).

25 Allow the mud to sit for 10 or 15 minutes so the surface has begun to dry.

26 Take a car-window squeegee and wet it thoroughly using a spray bottle filled with water (photo X).

27 Wipe the squeegee over the partially dried mud to smooth it out, gradually removing high and low spots, feathering out any ridges, and creating an even finish (photo Y). When the squeegee stops moving easily over the surface, wet it again with the sprayer. You can also spray water directly onto the mud.

28 Allow the mud to fully dry, repeat the application and rewetting process as necessary, and, when the final coat is dry, paint the wall to match the surrounding wall (photo Z).

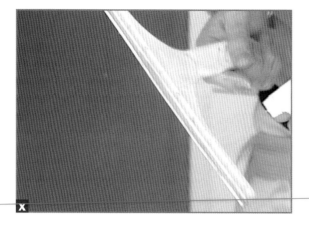

BASEBOARD TRIM

1 Purchase baseboard trim that matches the existing baseboards in each room, and pre-paint it to match the trim colors in those spaces.

2 Measure the gaps in the baseboard, and cut the new material to length using a miter saw.

3 Install the baseboard by driving 3-inch finish nails into the new wall studs and bottom plate (photo A).

4 Putty the nail holes, and caulk the top edge of the baseboard and the joints where they meet the old pieces. Allow these fillers to dry.

5 Touch up the paint on the trim and the walls where necessary.

BUDGET MAKEOVER

Tim and Heidi's bedroom was a decorating disaster. The faux-wood plastic laminate furniture was nearly 40 years old, the walls were pockmarked from an old wallpaper removal gone awry, and the whole place was devoid of color or character. But the busy couple didn't know how to give the space what it needed without spending a fortune.

BEFORE: The old bedroom suffered from bland white walls and dated laminate furniture that had once belonged to Heidi's parents.

AFTER: Color-washed walls, new beadboard wainscot, and a few coats of paint on the old furniture have transformed the bedroom into a relaxing getaway for the Bensons.

PROJECT SUMMARY

This job entailed numerous projects that any handy homeowners can tackle for themselves.

Installing Beadboard Wainscot. Wainscot is woodwork that covers only the lower third of the wall and lends variety to the room. Installing it is fairly simple, if you use sheets of beadboard paneling.

Glazing Walls. This simple decorative painting technique brings color and visual interest to the walls, hiding the damaged finish and making artwork unnecessary.

Painting Laminate Furniture. You can update old plastic laminate furniture with specialty paints designed to adhere to slick surfaces.

Building a Headboard. Amy Devers has a novel technique for making a great new headboard using salvaged house parts.

AFTER: The headboard Amy built is actually made from old house parts—a door and crown molding—plus a little ingenuity.

A

B

C

You Will Need

Utility knife	⅜" drill bit
Flat bar	Jigsaw
Hammer	2½" finish nails
Nippers	Caulk gun
Screwdriver set	Panel adhesive
Tape measure and pencil	1½" finish nails
¼" beadboard paneling	Nail set
4' level	Pneumatic nail gun
Electronic stud finder	Chair rail molding
Circular saw	Baseboard
Quick-lock clamps	Painter's caulk
Drill/driver	Electric box extenders

INSTALLING BEADBOARD WAINSCOT

Wainscot got its start as a way to protect the part of a wall that's most likely to get damaged by dining room furniture or bathroom splashes, but it's now chosen mostly for its pleasing visual effect.

1 Use a utility knife to cut the old paint along the baseboards, and then use a flat bar and a hammer (photo A) to remove the moldings without damaging them (photo B). Use nippers to remove the nails from the old molding by pulling them out from the back side.

2 Remove the face plates from the electrical outlets by using a flat head screw driver to back out the screws that hold them (photo C).

3 With the power shut off to all of the circuits in the room, remove the outlets from the boxes by backing out the screws, and allow them to hang by their wires.

4 Measure from the floor to the height for the new wainscot, which for this project was 32 inches (photo D). This size allows for three strips of wainscot to be cut from each 4x8 sheet of ¼-inch thick beadboard paneling. The last piece will be slightly short because of the width of the saw blade from the two cuts, but the gap will be covered by baseboard.

5 Transfer the height of your wainscot around the room using a 4-foot level (photo E).

6 Use an electronic stud finder to locate the studs in the walls (photo F), and mark them with a pencil.

7 Measure for the first board, making sure that it will end at the midpoint of a wall stud, so that the ends are well secured. Use quick-lock clamps to fasten a 4-foot level to the panel to guide your circular saw as you make the cuts, working from the back side of the panel. (photo G).

8 To cut out for an electrical outlet, measure from the level line and the nearest side of the outlet (photo H), and transfer those measurements to the beadboard. Use a drill with a bit that's bigger than your jigsaw blade to make a hole at each corner of the cutout you will make (photo I). Flip the beadboard over, and use the jigsaw to connect the holes and produce the rectangular opening (photo J).

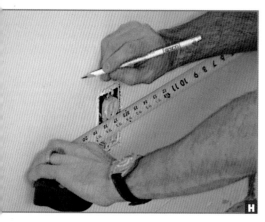

9 To make a cutout for a window, first check the window molding under the sill. If it's a complex shape, use a flat bar to carefully remove it, and use nippers to pull the nails from the back side. It will get reinstalled with 2½-inch finishing nails over the top of the beadboard. Then use the tape measure to determine the dimension of the cutout you need. Or, hold the panel in position, mark the cuts (photo K), transfer the measurements to the board, and cut using a drill to make the corner and a jigsaw to cut the lines.

10 Place the cut piece into position, and test the fit. Then, lay the piece face down, and use a caulk gun to apply panel adhesive to the back. Draw a line of adhesive around the perimeter and any openings, and a zigzag pattern through the middle (photo L).

11 Place the glued panel into position, making sure to keep it flush with the level line.

12 Fasten the panel every six inches along every stud using 1½-inch finish nails, a hammer, and a nail set to sink the heads. Or use a pneumatic nail gun, which will greatly reduce the chances of marring the surface with an errant hammer blow.

13 Once all of the paneling is installed, replace any window molding that was removed (photo M).

14 Measure and cut chair-rail molding to sit on top of the wainscot following the instructions on page 210-211.

15 Nail the molding into the wall studs, using the nail holes in the wainscot as a guide.

16 Cut and install the baseboard, either using the old material or new stock and following the same process used for the cap molding.

17 Fill all nail holes with painter's caulk, using your finger to smooth it out (photo N).

18 Reattach the electrical outlets to their boxes, using box extenders (available at electrical supply stores) if needed to ensure that the outlet is flush with the paneling.

19 Next, paint the wainscot. When the paint is dry, reattach the electrical cover plates (or install new ones).

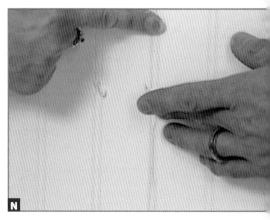

You Will Need

Blue painter's tape	Paint rollers
Drop cloth	Base color paint
Fine-grit sandpaper	Top color paint
Sanding head	Wallpaper paste
Scrap plywood or drywall	Paint pot
Paintbrushes	4" polyester-bristle paintbrush

GLAZING WALLS

Here's an easy fix for old walls that have been pockmarked by wallpaper removal, poor spackling repairs, or holes left behind from pictures and shelves that have been removed. Camouflage the imperfections by glazing the walls, a decorative painting technique that brings a multicolored texture to the walls.

1 A color wash involves applying two different colors of paint, a base coat and then a thin glaze. The glaze is a thin second coat in a different color—it's typically darker than the first and can either be similar in color or very different, your choice. You can find assistance with choosing colors at any good paint store.

2 Use blue painter's tape to mask off the edges of the area to be painted (photo A), and lay a drop cloth on the floor. These steps will protect adjacent surfaces from drips and spills.

3 Use fine-grit sandpaper loaded into a sanding head to lightly scuff the entire surface that will be painted (photo B).

4 Practice the following process on a scrap piece of plywood or drywall to perfect your technique before trying it out on your walls.

5 Apply the base coat, which is typically the lighter color, using paintbrushes for the edges of the walls and a roller for the middle (photo C). Allow the base coat to dry thoroughly.

6 In a plastic paint pot, mix equal parts of the accent color paint and wallpaper paste to create the glaze (photo D).

7 Use a 4-inch, polyester-bristle paint brush to apply the glaze to the wall (photo E). Use arcing, wavy strokes instead of straight, even ones.

8 When the glaze is tacky, but not yet dry, brush it with a dry paint brush. This removes some of the finish, exposing the color underneath.

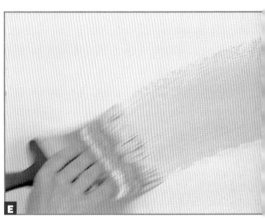

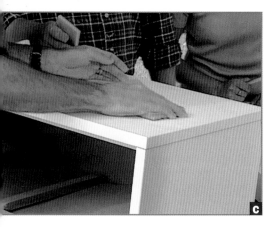

You Will Need

Drop cloths	Vapor masks
Fine-grit sandpaper	Spray laminate primer
Paint thinner	Satin spray paint
Rags	Antiquing kit (optional)

PAINTING LAMINATE FURNITURE

The hand-me-down furniture in Tim and Heidi's bedroom was 30 to 40 years old, and its plastic faux-wood grain was definitely out of date. To bring the pieces into the 21st century, the *DIY to the Rescue* crew showed the homeowners how to paint the shiny surfaces.

1 Set the furniture on drop cloths in a shady spot outside on the driveway.

2 Prepare the surfaces by sanding with fine grit sandpaper, and then use rags to rub them down with paint thinner (photo A).

3 Wearing vapor masks, spray all of the surfaces with laminate primer (photo B). Once the primer is dry, sand lightly with fine-grit sandpaper.

4 Spray-paint all surfaces with satin paint in your choice of color, sand lightly when dry (photo C), and repeat with a second coat of paint—or with an antiquing glaze, if you prefer.

You Will Need

Ladder-style panel door	1x4
Crown molding	1½" finish nails
Screwdriver set	Nail set
Tape measure	Pneumatic nail gun or hammer
Circular saw	2x4 boards
4' level	2x2 boards
Quick-lock clamps	3" screws
¾" plywood	Wood putty
Jigsaw	Primer and paint
1½" wood screws	Electronic stud finder
Drill/driver	Ratchet set
2x6 boards	Lag bolts
Miter saw	

BUILDING A HEADBOARD

A newly painted finish wouldn't solve the Benson's biggest complaint about their headboard—it's for a full-sized bed, which was too small for them. So, after the *DIY to the Rescue* team gave the couple a new queen-size mattress set, Amy Devers showed Tim a simple trick for making a new headboard from salvaged house parts.

1 The main ingredients for this project are an old ladder-style panel door and crown molding, both of which you can find at architectural salvage yards (photo A, right).

2 Remove any hinges, knobs, or other hardware by backing out the screws.

3 Measure the width of your bed (in this case, 60 inches), and cut the old door (this one was 84 inches) down to the bed's size. Plan so that you don't just cut the excess off of one end. Arrange cuts from both sides that will give the remaining section a pleasing visual symmetry. Mark cut lines through the door's rails, not its panels.

4 Use quick lock clamps to fasten a 4-foot level to the door as a straightedge to guide your circular saw as you make each cut (photo B). You'll need to measure the saw's base plate following the instructions on pages 49-50, steps 8-9.

5 Cut a piece of ¾-inch plywood to serve as a hidden U-shaped support structure for the door: Use a circular saw and jigsaw to cut it to the full length of the door, and then notch out for two 5½-inch-wide, 24-inch-long legs.

6 Align it on the backside of your new headboard (photo C), and fasten it to the stiles and rails of the door using 1½-inch wood screws and a drill/driver (photo D).

7 Cut two 24-inch lengths of 2x6 boards using either a circular saw or miter saw, and hold them against the plywood legs. Fasten them with the wood screws through the plywood (photo E).

8 Cut two 1x4 boards to a few inches longer than the height of your new headboard, using a miter saw set at a 45-degree angle (photo F). Position them on either side of the headboard, with the miter at the top, and make a mark at the bottom of the leg (photo G). Put a square cut at those marks.

9 Attach the sides to the door using 1½-inch finish nails and either a hammer and nail set or a pneumatic nail gun.

REMOVING OLD PAINT

If you're purchasing your new door and molding from a salvage yard, ask the seller about dip-stripping it. That's a paint removal process that many house parts sellers can do quickly and affordably, and it'll make refinishing the piece easier for you.

10 Measure between the two trim pieces (photo H, previous page) and cut a top piece with miters at both ends. (Make it a hair too long, and shave it down to fit by cutting again to ensure a perfect fit.)

11 Make two supports for the crown molding by nailing 2-foot lengths of 2x4 and 2x2 into an L-shape (photo I). Use 3-inch screws to attach these to either end of the door as shown (photo J).

12 Cut a length of the salvaged crown molding with mitered ends to fit across the door. Cut mitered caps for each end (photo K) and fasten them in place with finish nails.

13 Cut a 1x4 to size and finish nail it to the top of the crown molding to ensure a functional shelf on the headboard (photo L).

14 Fill the nail and screw holes with putty. Then, prime and paint.

15 To install the headboard, find studs in the wall using an electronic stud finder. Drill holes about ½-inch

deep in those locations to serve as countersinks and then drill narrower holes through the headboard and drywall or plaster and slightly into the wall studs (photo M).

16 Insert lag bolts into the holes and use a ratchet set to tighten them down.

WINDOW DRESSING

Because Ron's 24-year-old son, Justin, has special needs, he lives in his father's home. The family wanted to transform a portion of their house into a mini-apartment where Justin could lead a semi-independent life. Their plan was to convert an extra room alongside Justin's bedroom into a comfortable living room, complete with a snack bar and mini-refrigerator, and to create an open floor plan feeling between the two rooms.

BEFORE: The family wanted to link this extra room to Justin's bedroom in order to give it an apartment-like feel.

AFTER: A frosted glass door and two homemade sidelights provide a bright and open connection to Justin's bedroom.

PROJECT SUMMARY

The *DIY to the Rescue* crew connected the bedroom and living room with a new French-style glass door, the process for which can be seen on pages 189-191. They built a custom entertainment center for Justin's three televisions and his video games. They also installed a small countertop with cabinets and a mini-refrigerator underneath, so that Justin can make his own snacks and small meals.

Making a Custom Window. The crew also installed two sidelight windows alongside the French door to help create an open feel to the adjacent rooms. These windows were built on site. Following these steps, instead of ordering custom units for your project, can save you a lot of money.

You Will Need

⅛" Plexiglas	1" finish nails
1x6 clear pine	Hammer and nailset
½x½" pine (optional)	Pneumatic nail gun (optional)
Tape measure	1⅝" finish nails or drywall screws
Table saw with rip fence	Drill
Miter saw	Glass-scoring tool
Combination square and pencil	Framing square
Wood glue	

MAKING A CUSTOM WINDOW

Constructing a simple picture window or sidelight window from scratch is a lot easier than you might think, and doing it yourself can save a bunch of money (photo A).

1 Measure the thickness of the wall, from the face of the drywall on one side to the face of the drywall on the opposite side. (A standard wall, made of 2x4s and drywall, is 4½-inches thick.)

2 Use a table saw with a rip fence to cut down 1x6 stock to 4½ inches (photo B), or to the thickness of your wall, which may require a different size of lumber stock. This will be the window jamb.

3 Rip scrap material to a ½-x½-inch size (or purchase stock ½x½-inch material). These will be the stops, which will eventually hold the glass in the window (Photo C).

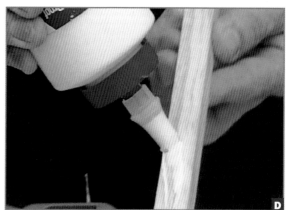

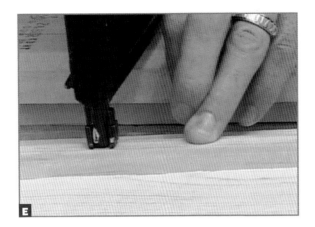

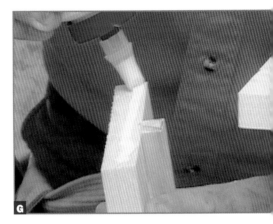

4 Measure the height and width of the window opening. Use a miter saw to cut two vertical sides from the 4½-inch boards. Make the dimension ½ inch smaller than the window height to allow you to maneuver the window slightly during installation, so you can make it plumb and level. And make the cuts standard 90-degree crosscuts.

5 Next, cut the horizontal top and bottom pieces. To figure the measurement, subtract 2 inches from the width of the window opening. This will provide ½ inch of wiggle room for plumbing and leveling purposes, and it will accommodate the ¾-inch thickness of each side piece, which will overlap the top and bottom.

6 Cut eight pieces of ½x½ material, two for each of the four jamb pieces, making the ones for the horizontal jambs match their jamb's length and making the vertical stops 2½ inches shorter than their jambs (to accommodate the overlapping horizontal jambs and stops).

7 Set a combination square to half the width of the jamb minus ¹⁄₁₆ inch (2³⁄₁₆ inches for a 4½-inch jamb) and use it to guide a pencil along each jamb to mark a line.

8 Use wood glue (photo D) and 1-inch finish nails to attach one ½x½ inch piece to each jamb section, setting it on the pencil line (photo E). You can do this with a hammer and nailset or with a pneumatic nail gun. For the vertical jambs, center the stops on the board, so that there's a 1¼-inch gap on each end.

9 Assemble the four jambs together, making sure to align the stops properly on the interior of the frame (photo F). Use glue on each joint (photo G), as well as either 1⅝-inch finish nails (photo H) or, better, 1⅝-inch drywall screws in predrilled holes.

10 Measure between the inside edges of the jambs to determine the size for the glass (photo I).

11 You can order standard window glass, frosted glass, or even stained glass from a glass shop. Or, do what Karl and Ron did here and use ⅛-inch Plexiglas, which is an acrylic product that you can easily cut yourself and isn't nearly as precarious to work with as real glass.

12 Transfer the height measurements to each edge of the Plexiglas using a glass scoring tool (photo J).

13 Connect the marks with a straightedge, such as a framing square, and score the plastic several times with the scoring tool (photo K).

14 Align the scored line over the edge of your work surface, hold the straight edge on top of its good side, and snap the Plexiglas along the line (photo L).

15 Repeat steps 13 through 14 for the width of the window.

16 Use your fingers to peel the protective film from the glass (photo M), and lay the glass into the frame, making sure it's on the same side of the stops as your pencil line (photo N).

17 Glue up the remaining stops and position them over the glass to sandwich it in place. Use a hammer to tap in the stops if necessary. Fasten the stops with the 1-inch finish nails.

18 Install and trim out the window following the steps beginning on page 243.

SMOOTH MOVES

Home improvements require more than just good homeowners. Scott and his wife Martini learned the hard way, after ripping down the ugly 1970's wall paneling in their bedroom, only to discover that the plaster walls underneath had been wrecked by the glue holding up the paneling. So their makeover project stalled until the *DIY to the Rescue* team arrived.

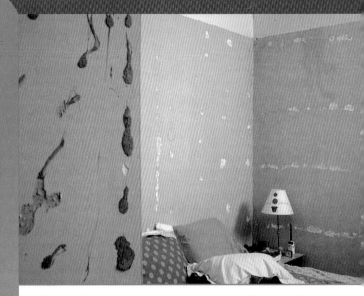

Before: The bedroom walls were pockmarked with damage from removing some old 1970's paneling, and the space felt cramped because of a closet that jutted into the room at the left side of this photo.

After: The closet is gone, and smooth walls, new crown molding, and fresh paint have transformed the space. A new wardrobe armoire makes up for the lost storage.

PROJECT SUMMARY

The problems in Martini and Scott's bedroom are very common. And understanding how to solve them can give any homeowners the ammunition they need to solve similar dilemmas in their homes.

Removing a Closet. A previous homeowner had added a closet to the bedroom, but, although the extra storage was convenient, the closet jutted into the bedroom making the space feel cramped.

Repairing Rough Walls. Whatever has caused dings and dents in a wall, as long as the wallboard or plaster is sound and the damage doesn't completely penetrate the wall, the problems can be smoothed out with spackle and joint compound.

Installing Crown Molding. Like a crown that sits on top of the room, this trim covers the joint where the ceiling meets the walls, and it can lend a sense of height and drama to any room.

REMOVING A CLOSET

This closet was added by a previous homeowner to provide extra wardrobe storage, but it jutted out from the wall (photo A), cramping the bedroom space and feeling out of sync with the house's 1940's floor plan. So, Amy donned a dust mask and goggles and showed the homeowners how to demolish it.

You Will Need

Hammer

Flat bar

Crow bar

Reciprocating saw

Nail nippers

A

1 Remove the closet doors, shelf, and pole (photo B), and use a hammer and flat bar to pry all the wood trim off of the interior and exterior of the closet (photo C).

2 Hit the closet wall with a hammer a few times to punch a line of holes across the center of the wallboard (photo D). This weakens the material and gives you a place to grab it and pull it off of the studs. Where necessary, use the flat bar and a crow bar to help pry all of the wallboard free.

3 Slice through each of the wall studs using a reciprocating saw (photo E). Pull out the studs, using the crow bar and hammer when necessary.

4 With all of the wall framing gone, use nail nippers to remove any nails that are still sticking out of the floor, ceiling, and adjacent walls.

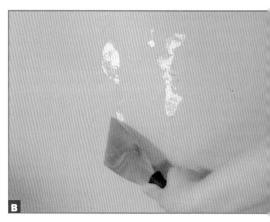

REPAIRING ROUGH WALLS

After removing old wall paneling—and the tough construction adhesive that held it in place—the homeowners found their bedroom walls covered with damage (photo A). But the old plaster walls were still solid, so they didn't require removal or covering over with new wallboard. All they needed were some spot repairs. And the following process works well for fixing any superficial wall damage.

You Will Need

Putty knife	Taping knife
Paint scraper	Fine grit sandpaper
Heavy-duty drill	Dust masks
Mixer blade attachment	Safety glasses
Lightweight spackling compound	Joint compound
5-gallon bucket	Pole sander
Taping tray or hawk	

1 Remove any remaining glue, old wallpaper, or other debris by running a putty knife or a paint scraper over the surface (photo B).

2 Use a mixer blade attachment in a heavy-duty drill to combine a batch of lightweight spackling compound with water in a 5 gallon bucket (photo C). Add the water gradually until it has the consistency of cake batter (photo D). Don't make too much at a time, or it'll begin to cure before you apply it and become very difficult to work with. (Adding more water won't help.)

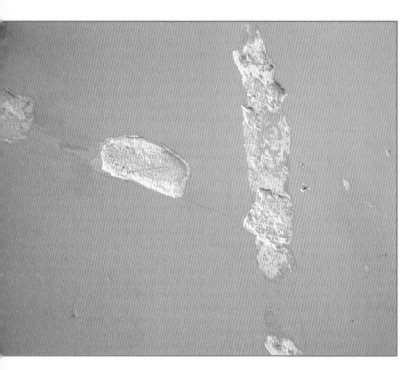

MIXING JOINT COMPOUND

Use cool water when mixing joint compound because warm water will accelerate the curing process and give you less time to work with the material before it hardens.

3 Allow the mixture to stand for one minute, and then mix it again, adding water as needed until it's the consistency of frosting. The pause gives the powder a chance to absorb the moisture and starts the chemical reaction that causes it to cure rock hard.

4 Take a couple of scoops of compound from the bucket with your putty knife and place it into a taping tray or hawk. Then, use the knife to apply it to each damaged section of the wall, pushing the material into the indentation (photo E). Then, use the knife's edge to scrape it flush with the finished surface (photo F).

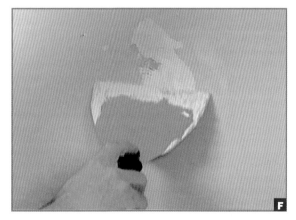

5 Allow the compound to dry completely, following the timing listed on the product bag, and then sand out any high spots with fine-grit sandpaper while wearing a dust mask and safety glasses.

6 Check your results. Because the filler shrinks as it dries, you'll need to apply another coat, by repeating steps 2 through 5, if the indentations are deeper than ⅛ inch. If they're not, it's ready for the finish coat.

7 Apply premixed joint compound using a 5-inch wide putty knife. Don't scrape the material flush with the surface this time, however. Instead, lay a thin coating over each damaged spot and use the knife to taper the coating's edges back to the wall, a process called feathering, which greatly reduces the amount of sanding needed later (photo G).

8 Allow the joint compound to dry overnight, and then load fine-grit sandpaper onto a pole sander (photo H), and sand the entire wall to remove any uneven spots or ridges. Then, the walls are ready for paint.

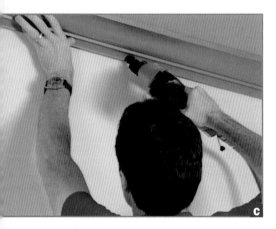

INSTALLING CROWN MOLDING

Crown molding requires fairly advanced DIY carpentry skills because you'll need to make some tricky cuts to get the pieces to form nice tight joints at the corners. Still, it looks a lot harder than it really is.

You Will Need	
Primer and paint	Hammer and nail set
Paintbrushes	Pneumatic trim nail gun
Crown molding	Coping saw
Electronic stud finder	Safety glasses
Tape measure	Wood glue
Compound miter saw	Wood putty
2½" finish nails	Acrylic caulk

1 Before installation, prime and paint the crown molding and paint the walls and ceiling too (photo A). That'll save you a lot of delicate painting work later, when you will need to avoid getting one color of paint onto another surface.

2 Use an electronic stud finder to locate the framing members in the wall and ceiling so that you can nail the crown molding into them, which is essential for fastening it securely and for avoiding open seams. On this project, however, there's wood lath behind the plaster walls and ceiling, which eliminates the need for this step because there's plenty of nailing material behind the plaster.

3 Measure the location for the first piece of molding, and cut a single length to fit the space using a compound miter saw. Standard square cuts should be used for this first piece (photo B), but you'll need the adjustability of this tool for later cuts.

4 Set the first piece into position so that one flange sits flush on the ceiling and the other sits flush on the wall. Then fasten it in place with 2½-inch finish nails through those flanges and into the framing that you've marked (or into the lath). You can use a hammer for this (with a nail set to sink the heads), but it's easier to rent a pneumatic nail gun because it'll speed up the job and greatly reduce the risk of marring the woodwork as you go (photo C).

CROWN MOLDING JOINTS

If you can't get crown molding in lengths long enough for one or more of your walls (or can't get such long pieces home), you'll need to create a joint. Locate the seam over a wall stud or ceiling joist, so that both ends can be fastened firmly in place, and to use matching 45-degree bevel cuts, which will hide the joint better than square cuts.

5 Measure for the next piece and cut it to length, but this time, don't make a square cut. For the edge that will meet the already-installed molding, set your compound miter saw to a 34⅝-degrees miter (the horizontal adjustment on the saw) and a 31⅜-degree bevel (the vertical adjustment on the saw). This is the standard cut for crown molding (photo D). The blade should taper out from the measurement point.

6 After this cut, use a coping saw to carefully follow the profile of the front edge of the angled cut you made on the miter saw (photo E). This will produce an edge that aligns perfectly with the adjoining crown molding.

7 Install the coped piece, and then repeat the process for the next wall, creating mitered and coped cuts wherever a new board will meet an already installed one.

8 For outer corners—corners that point into the room—cut both pieces using the same miter and bevel measurements that you used for the inside corners. But, this time, the blade should taper in from the measurement point. And do not cope these cuts. Once you've test-fit both pieces, use small finish nails and glue to lock the two mitered edges tightly together before installing them.

9 Apply acrylic caulk along the top and bottom of the crown molding and along all joints to help hide any irregularities (photo F). Fill the nail holes with wood putty, and then touch up the paint as necessary.

WALL TO WALL

Although their bathroom leak had long since been fixed, and the leaked water had long since dried, the wall-to-wall carpeting in Brad and Paula's bedroom had become permanently musty and mildewed from the moisture. It was so bad that Brad had actually cut out the damaged area with a utility knife, leaving the concrete floor exposed in a portion of their bedroom. The couple needed help installing a new, full-sized carpet—as well as doing some drywall repairs and hanging crown molding.

PROJECT SUMMARY

You can learn the ins and outs of drywall repair (pages 27 and 28) and hanging crown molding (pages 142 and 143) elsewhere in this book. It's the floor project we'll focus on here.

Installing Wall-to-Wall Carpeting. There's nothing like wall-to-wall carpeting with a thick pad underneath to make a bedroom warm, cozy, and comfortable. And you can save some money by installing the carpet yourself.

BEFORE: The family had removed a portion of their old bedroom carpet that was ruined by a bathroom leak.

AFTER: The new carpeting, as well as some new paint and a new crown molding, has warmed up the room considerably.

INSTALLING WALL-TO-WALL CARPET

You can install carpeting over virtually any floor, as long as it's stable, dry, and flat. And the job is easy once you understand how it's done.

You Will Need

Carpet	Scissors or utility knife
Carpet padding	Carpet adhesive (for a concrete subfloor)
Wallpaper scraper	Masking tape
Broom or vacuum	Row finder
Tape measure	Loop pile cutter
Tackless strip	Knee kicker
Miter, circular, or hand saw	Carpet knife
Hammer	Stair tool

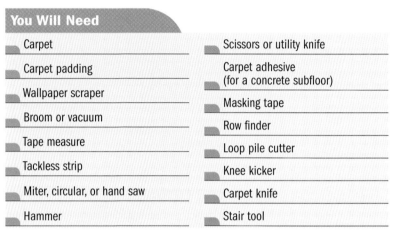

1 Roll out the carpet on a clean, flat surface outside in the sunshine (photo A). The warmth of the sun will help to flatten out the fibers, which have been rolled up for a long time, and you'll also get the chance to trim the carpet to rough size, which will simplify the installation.

2 Remove the shoe-molding, which is the strip of molding at the bottom edge of the baseboard in some houses.

3 Tear out any old flooring materials, such as carpeting or linoleum. Then use a sharp wallpaper scraper, as well as a push broom or vacuum, to remove any debris clean the floor completely (photo B).

4 Lay tackless strips around the perimeter of the room about ¼ inch from the wall, cutting the strips as needed using a miter saw, circular saw, or hand saw. Arrange the strips so that the teeth angle toward the wall and fasten them in place using the nails provided with them (photo C).

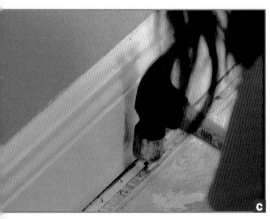

5 Measure the length and width of the room, including alcoves, entryways, thresholds, and closets (photo D). Add 4 inches to both dimensions so the carpet will be slightly oversized at first. You can make the final cuts when it's in place.

6 Roll out padding (photo E) along the strip adjacent to one wall, making sure the plastic weave of the padding is on top because this allows the carpet to be moved while you're installing it.

7 Use a utility knife or scissors to cut the padding so that it lays just inside the tackless strip.

8 For a concrete subfloor like this one, it's a good idea to use a little carpet adhesive to help stick down the padding. Working on one half of the strip at a time, roll the padding back to the mid-point of the floor (photo F), and pour a thin bead of adhesive onto the floor in a zigzag pattern (photo G) before replacing the pad. Then roll back the other side of the padding, pour the glue, and put it back in place.

9 Repeat steps 6 through 8 for additional strips of padding until the floor is covered with padding.

TIPS | DIY Network Home Improvement

OUT OF THE WAY

Always remove any doors before laying down carpet because they'll get in your way as you try to position the carpet. If you need to cut them down later, see pages 166-169.

10 Cover all of the seams between strips of padding with masking tape (photo H).

11 Transfer the overall measurements to the carpet and cut it to rough size. You can do this by working from the back and using a carpet knife and a long straightedge, but you'll get a neater job with a couple of inexpensive specialty tools: A row finder creates a straight line between the pile so you won't need a straightedge and can cut between the carpet fibers rather than through them (photo I). And a loop pile cutter makes quick work of cutting the carpet from the top (photo J).

12 Roll up the carpet, bring it inside, and unroll it in the proper orientation for the room.

13 To stretch the rug tightly over the floor and lock it onto the barbs of the tackless strip, you'll need a tool called a knee kicker. To use it, first turn the dial so that the teeth are the exact thickness of the rug's pile (photo K).

14 Starting along a short edge of the carpet, place the knee kicker at one corner of the carpet, press the teeth into the carpet, and whack the other end of the tool with your knee (photo L). This will stretch the carpet and lock it onto the tackless strip.

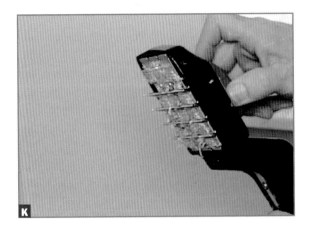

15 Move 6 inches or so from the corner and repeat the process, and keep moving across the wall, until you've completed the entire wall.

16 Fold the excess carpet down, press it into the corner where the floor meets the wall, and slice it using a carpet knife (photo M).

17 Make another pass along the wall with your knee kicker to ensure that the carpet is positioned properly. As you go, tuck the loose edge of the carpet down behind the tackless strip with a stair tool, which is like a big, dull chisel (photo N).

18 Repeat steps 14 through 17 for the opposite wall, and then for the long walls.

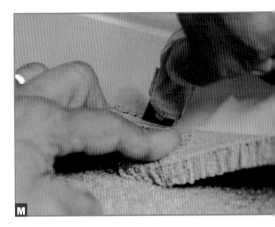

4

Kids' Rooms

Although organization and safety are often the main reasons parents start a kids' room remodel, it's also a great chance to discover more about your child's passions and integrate them in the room's decor. Start by asking the child about his or her favorite toys, games, sports, animals, and colors; then, brainstorm ways to incorporate their ideas into the remodel. Next, give some thought to practical considerations such as childproof materials (easy-to-clean paints and carpets, for instance), safety, and plenty of storage space for all those toys and clothes. Now, when you send the kids to their rooms, they'll be happy to go!

KID SPACE

Homeowners Trish and Gabriel had emptied their twin sons' bedroom of furniture and embarked on a redecorating project months before the *DIY to the Rescue* team arrived on the scene. The room was still a construction zone because the couple couldn't get the wallpaper off the wall, no matter how much chemical stripper they used.

Before: The couple had started stripping an ancient wallpaper border, but gave up because the job was so difficult. They found themselves gouging the walls in the process.

After: New carpet tiles complement a new paint job and contrast the new, light-colored furniture.

PROJECT SUMMARY

Wallpaper stripping was only the beginning. This rescue involved three projects that the homeowners completed themselves after learning the ropes from Amy and Karl.

Stripping Wallpaper. The secret to stripping stubborn paper isn't elbow grease. It's perforating the paper so the stripping solution can get at the old adhesive.

Installing a Closet-Organizing System. Here's how to put up a basic modular system that will allow you to place shelves, hooks, cubbies, bins, hangers, and drawers anywhere you want them.

Laying Carpet Tile. Carpet tiles? That's right. These squares of carpeting are easy to install, easy to change later, and come in lots of great contemporary designs.

Before: The double-wide closet had a generous amount of space for the twins' clothes and toys, but most of it was going to waste.

After: The modular closet system allows the homeowners to arrange various storage components however they want and to rearrange them as the kids' needs change.

A

B

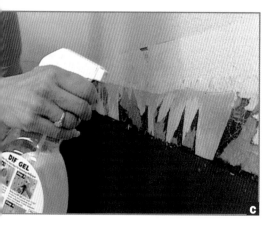

C

You Will Need

White vinegar	Wallpaper scraper
Warm water	Sponge
Wallpaper scoring tool	TSP substitute painter's detergent
Waterproof gloves	Fine-grit sanding block
Safety glasses	Joint compound
Spray bottle	Taping knife

STRIPPING WALLPAPER

If wallpaper is relatively recent, it should peel away easily because newer glues are more forgiving. In fact, if it's a vinyl wallpaper, each strip may simply pull off in a whole sheet once you peel up a corner. For older papers, though, the glues are tenacious and the paper easily shreds into tiny shards as you scrape it. In this case, the job is an old wallpaper border, but the following procedure works just as well for entire walls.

1 The secret of stripping wallpaper is to deactivate the adhesive rather than battle it with elbow grease. You can use a chemical stripper, a wallpaper steamer, or a simple homemade solution made up of equal parts white vinegar and warm water, as was done here.

2 Roll a wallpaper scoring tool over the surface of the paper (photo A). This essential tool is an inexpensive paint-shop product that has little teeth to perforate the paper (photo B), which allows the stripping solution to penetrate and go to work on the adhesive behind it.

3 Load the homemade stripping solution into a spray bottle and, wearing waterproof gloves and safety glasses, spritz it onto the perforated paper (photo C), making sure to wet the paper thoroughly.

4 Wait 15 minutes to allow the solution to work.

5 Use a sharp wallpaper scraper to separate the wallpaper from the wall (photo D). Be careful not to tear the drywall paper underneath.

6 Once the paper is completely removed, use a sponge to wash away any remaining stripping solution with TSP substitute (a painter's detergent that you mix with water).

7 Allow the area to dry and then sand it lightly with a fine-grit sanding block (photo E).

8 Use a taping knife to apply a very thin layer of joint compound over any tears, pocks, or gouges (photo F).

You can choose a fast-drying product to speed up the process.

9 Once the joint compound is dry, sand lightly again with the sanding block, and inspect the results to see whether another coat of compound is needed. Repeat as necessary.

10 After the final coat is sanded, the walls are ready for paint.

A

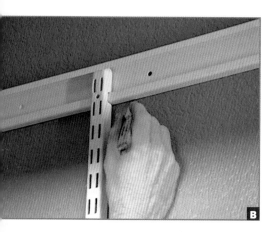

B

C

INSTALLING A CLOSET-ORGANIZING SYSTEM

You don't need to hire a contractor to install a closet-organizing system. You can do it yourself with modular parts purchased at a home center or specialty shop. Here are the basic steps for one common product type.

You Will Need

Modular metal closet system	Tape measure and pencil
Hammer and nails	Torpedo level
Flat bar	Electronic stud finder
Vinyl spackle	Drill/driver
Fine-grit sanding block	3" wood screws
Paint and rollers or brushes	1" drywall screws

1 Temporarily remove the closet door or doors by lifting them off of their tracks or pulling the hinge pins by setting a nail against their bottoms and striking it with a hammer.

2 Remove any old closet shelving and poles, and then use a flat bar and hammer to pry off the cleats that supported them. Patch the wall using vinyl spackle and a sanding block if necessary (see pages 139-141).

3 Paint the closet. There's nothing like a fresh coat of paint to clean and brighten a closet, and you definitely want to paint before installing your organizing system, to simplify the job.

4 This entire modular system hangs from one horizontal bracket. To determine its height, position it on the wall and hang one of the vertical "standards" from it (photo A). Set the bracket so that the standard lands a couple inches above the baseboard, and make a pencil mark at that spot (photo B).

5 Holding the bracket on that mark, level it with a magnetic torpedo level (photo C) and draw a light pencil mark underneath it.

6 Use an electronic stud finder to locate the framing inside the wall, and mark stud locations with a pencil just below the level line.

7 Align the bracket so that its predrilled holes align with the wall studs. (In this case, there are predrilled holes located every 8 inches, so every other one can align with a stud.)

8 Fasten the bracket to the wall studs using 3-inch wood screws (photo D).

9 Measure the width of the closet and divide that in half to find the center point.

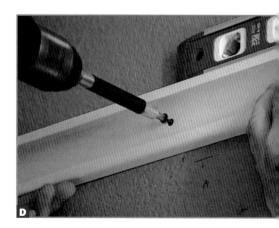

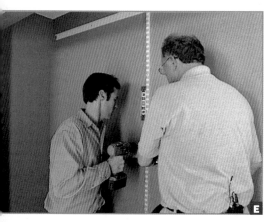

10 Hang the first standard on one side of the center point by placing it on the bracket, using the magnetic torpedo level to make sure it is plumb, and screwing it to the wall using 1-inch drywall screws (photo E). The screws need not hit a stud. They're not supporting any weight, just preventing lateral movement.

11 Install another standard in the same manner on the opposite side of the centerpoint (photo F).

12 Working from the center outward, locate and hang the remaining standards based on the size of your shelving (photo G).

13 Attach the shelving, drawers, cubbies, and other accessories sold with the kit (photo H).

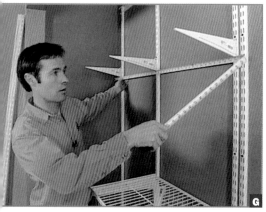

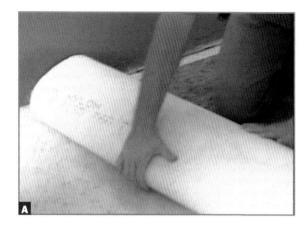

INSTALLING CARPET TILES

Like wall-to-wall carpeting, carpet tiles are a great way to bring warmth and coziness to a bedroom. Unlike wall-to-wall carpeting, these 20-inch squares make for an easy install-it-yourself job, and you can even replace a damaged square later if one is ruined by spills.

You Will Need

Gloves	Permanent marker
Flat bar	Framing square
Vacuum	Chalk line
Carpet tiles	Utility knife
Tape measure	

1 To remove old wall-to-wall carpeting, don heavy duty work gloves, start in a corner, and pull up on the carpet. Work a flat bar underneath if necessary, and pry the carpet up.

2 Roll up the carpet as you free it (photo A), and then roll up the padding that's underneath.

3 Use a flat bar to pry up the "tackless" strips around the perimeter of the room (photo B), being very careful of their sharp, protruding nails. Then, vacuum the floor thoroughly.

4 Measure one wall (photo C), divide its length in half, and then mark the midpoint on the floor using a permanent marker (photo D).

5 Use a framing square to measure the width of a tile, divide that in half, and make a center mark on the tile.

6 Place the tile against a wall, aligning its center with the wall's center (photo E). Then mark the floor on one side of the tile (photo F).

7 Use the marked tile to repeat this process on all four walls of the room. (If the room isn't a rectangle, you'll need to adjust this approach by following the instructions provided with the carpet.

8 Snap chalk lines between each matching set of marks on the opposite walls (photo G), and make a mark on the side of the lines that the midpoints are on.

9 Place the first carpet tile against one corner of the X that's marked on the floor (photo H). You can arrange the patterns on the tiles in a specific design or just lay them randomly, which was done here.

10 Add additional tiles along the chalk line, working from the center of the room toward a corner (photo I).

11 To cut a tile, flip it over and lay it in place (photo J). Use the permanent marker to make a mark on each side where the tile overlaps the adjacent tile (photo K). Lay the tile on a scrap board and hold a straight edge over the two marks (photo L). Run a sharp utility knife along the straight edge a few times to cut the rubber backing of the tile (photo M).

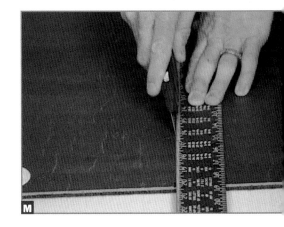

12 Once a quadrant of the floor is covered in tiles, check the alignment with the chalk lines and the spacing between the tiles (photo N).

13 Working from the middle of the room toward the corner, lift one tile at a time, peel off the backing, and press the tile into place (photo O).

14 Move to an adjacent quadrant of the floor and repeat the process, until the floor is complete.

15 Make sure to save any extra tiles because if any squares get damaged you can simply peel them up and stick down a new one—and you're assured of a good match if they're purchased at the same time.

NURSERY SCHOOL

Atlanta homeowners Tom and Nicole's youngest son's bedroom felt more like an extra room in the attic than it did like a little boy's bedroom. A makeshift door led to a storage room under the eaves, wintertime drafts made the room ice-cold, and the dormer-window alcove had become a messy staging area for baby toys and supplies.

BEFORE: Colby's bedroom was a dull and boring space, complete with a rough-cut plywood door leading to an adjacent storage room.

AFTER: Colorful walls, a wallpaper border, and bold star cutouts have brought life to the décor—and invisible repairs have made it a lot warmer and cozier too.

PROJECT SUMMARY

This job combined a host of different useful projects, from improving the room's energy efficiency to improving its color palette.

Cutting Down a Door. Before the crew could install a new pre-hung door to the adjacent storage room, they had to cut it down a few inches to fit under the eaves. Here's how to shrink a door.

Eliminating Drafts. A few easy-to-apply home center products can drastically reduce chilly drafts.

Building a Window Seat. This simple upholstered bench turns wasted space into the best seat in the house.

Hanging a Wallpaper Border. Here's an easy way to bring color and fun to a child's room.

An upholstered window seat has turned the alcove into a comfy spot for reading and playing—and it even doubles as a toy chest.

CUTTING DOWN A DOOR

You can see the steps for installing a pre-hung door on pages 276-279, but what do you do if your door opening is a little shorter than the available door sizes? Or, if you install new carpeting that requires taking a little something off the bottom of a door? The *DIY to the Rescue* crew showed Tom and Nicole how to cut down a door.

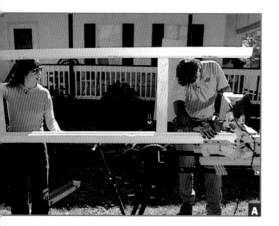

You Will Need

Tape measure and pencil	Brads
Miter saw	Hammer and nailset
Framing square	Pneumatic brad nailer (optional)
Utility knife	
Scrap trim	Sanding block
Quick-lock clamps	Medium-grit sandpaper
Circular saw	Fine-grit sandpaper
Flat bar	Manufacturer's touch-up paint (for a pre-finished door)
Wood glue	

1 Measure the height of the door opening, and then subtract about ¼ inch. This is the height for the jamb.

2 Pull the hinge pins to remove the pre-hung door from its jamb, position the jamb on your miter saw and cut each leg to length (photo A). You'll need a spotter to hold the jamb while you do the cutting.

3 Install the cut-down jamb into the opening following the instructions on pages 276-279.

4 Measure the distance between the top of the upper hinge and the floor. (Measuring from the hinge gives you a more accurate figure than measuring from the top of the jamb.)

5 Transfer the measurement to the door, again by measuring from the top of the upper hinge (photo B).

6 Use a framing square to draw a straight line for your cut (photo C) and then, while the square is still in place, score the line with a utility knife (photo D) to help protect the surface from blow-out damage when it's cut.

7 Use a piece of straight trim and two quick-lock clamps to make a fence that will guide your circular saw along the scored line (photo E). To do this, you'll need to measure the base plate on the circular saw and carefully position the straightedge accordingly (see page 49, step 8-9).

8 Use a circular saw to make the cut, keeping the baseplate flush against your homemade fence at all times (photo F).

9 If the bottom of the door is now hollow, your cut has completely removed the wood bottom rail from the door. This unseen structural piece gives weight and strength to the bottom of any hollow-core door, and you'll need to reinstall it.

10 Use a flat bar to pry the surface material from it or use your fingers to peel it away (photo G).

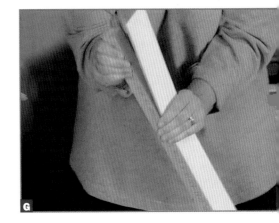

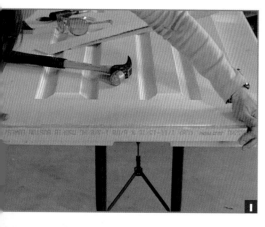

11 Apply wood glue to the wood rail and the inner surfaces of the door (photo H).

12 Insert the rail into the opening at the bottom of the door (photo I), being careful to line it up flush with the bottom edge by tapping it with a hammer (photo J).

13 Nail the rail into place using brads sunk through each face of the door. Use a hammer and nailset for this job or a pneumatic nail gun (photo K).

14 Use a sanding block with medium- and then fine-grit sandpaper to round over and smooth the cut edges.

15 If it's a pre-finished door, paint the bottom edge of the door and the nail heads, using paint provided by the manufacturer to match the finish.

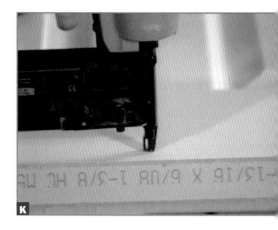

K

ELIMINATING DRAFTS

Drafts typically enter a room through the joints where different materials meet—such as where the drywall hits the floor, where the floor framing hits the wall framing, and around doors and windows. You can use the following techniques to close those gaps.

You Will Need

Spray foam insulation	Acrylic latex caulk	Outlet and light switch gaskets

A

OPEN FRAMING: Here's what to do in attics and basements—or when your walls are open for other home improvement projects: Fiberglass batts provide good insulation where the spaces between joists and studs are easily accessible. For tight and hard to reach places, however, apply spray foam insulation (photo A). The *DIY to the Rescue* team used commercial spraying equipment, but you can purchase spray cans of foam insulation at a home center.

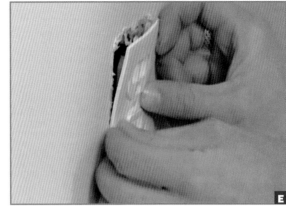

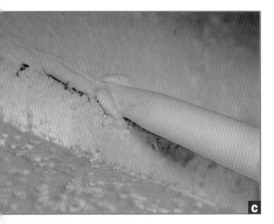

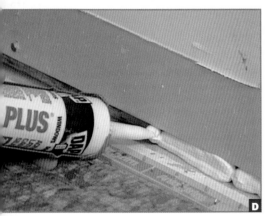

CEILING PENETRATIONS: On a cold day, if you run your hand around light fixtures and heat registers that are shut off, you may feel cold air pouring into the room. To block its easy entry, remove the register covers (photo B), light fixtures, and any other items that penetrate the ceiling. Then run a bead of acrylic latex caulk in the seam where the metal meets the drywall (photo C).

THE FLOOR-TO-WALL JOINT: You can also seal the seam where the subfloor meets the wall framing by temporarily removing the baseboards, and the wall-to-wall carpeting if necessary, and filling the space between the floor and the drywall with a heavy bead of acrylic latex caulk (photo D).

OUTLETS AND SWITCHES: Wherever outlets and switches are in exterior walls, there's also less insulation—or sometimes none at all. So electrical penetrations can be major sources of drafts. A simple solution is to install rubber insulation gaskets underneath the cover plates (photo E). Ask about the gaskets at a local electrical supply house.

BUILDING A WINDOW SEAT

Here's how to transform an awkward alcove into a cozy spot by installing a cushioned window seat with toy storage inside.

You Will Need

Flat bar	1x3
Tape measure and pencil	Miter or circular saw
1' level	1½" finish nails
Electronic stud finder	Hammer and nailset
¾" birch plywood	Pneumatic nail gun (optional)
Table saw	Piano hinge
2" drywall screws	1½" screws

1 Remove the baseboard from the alcove by carefully prying it free with a flat bar.

2 Measure up from the floor and mark the height for the window seat (minus about 4 inches for the thickness of the seat). Choose a height that's convenient for looking out of the window, but the seat on a standard dining or desk chair is about 18 inches off the ground for adults, and typically 12 to 15 inches high for children.

3 Use a 1-foot level to transfer the mark onto the three walls of the alcove (photo A).

4 Use an electronic stud finder to locate the wall framing (photo B) and mark the locations with pencil just above the level line.

5 Measure across the alcove and from the back wall to where you want the front edge of the seat. This, too, is a matter of preference, but a seat should be at least 16 or 18 inches deep to ensure that it's a comfortable perch for an adult.

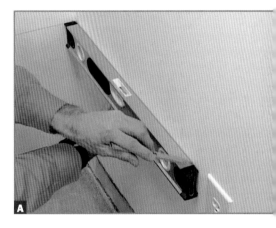

A

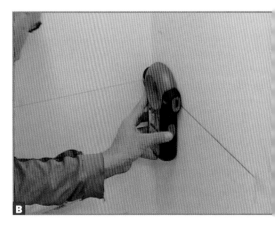

B

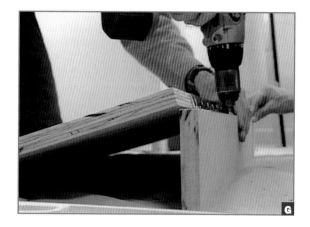

6 Cut ¾-inch birch plywood on a table saw to produce two pieces the height and depth of the seat (photo C).

7 Use 2-inch drywall screws to fasten these boards to the side walls, making sure to sink the screws into wall studs (photo D).

8 Cut a piece of 1x3—either using a miter or circular saw—to fit between the two plywood sides along the back wall of the alcove and fasten it into studs with 2-inch screws (photo E).

9 Using the table saw, cut a piece of the birch plywood for the front of the box, with its grain running horizontally across the face. Fasten it to the side pieces using 1½-inch finish nails (photo F). You can use a pneumatic nail gun or a hammer and nail set for this job.

10 For the top, cut a piece of 1x3 to fit across the rear of the box. Then, cut a piece of birch plywood to fit just in front of the 1x3 and cover the rest of the box, overlapping the front face by about ½ inch. It's grain should run front to back.

11 Join the 1x3 and plywood together using a piano hinge attached with 1½-inch screws into the edges of the plywood (photo G).

12 Fasten the 1x3 portion of the top to the 1x3 and plywood underneath it using the finishing nails. Leave the rest of the lid free to open and shut (photo H).

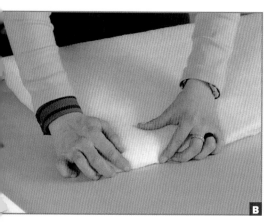

UPHOLSTERING THE BENCH

You Will Need

3" foam padding	Staples
Scissors	Decorative "show" fabric
½" plywood	Quick-lock clamps
Spray adhesive	1½" screws
Cotton batting	½x1" trim
Muslin	1" finish nails
Staple gun	

1 Use sharp scissors to cut a pad of 3-inch foam to the size of the pull-up lid. Then bevel the edge at a 45-degree angle all the way around the foam (photo A). This will give the foam a nice rounded edge when it's wrapped in fabric (photo B).

2 Cut a piece of ½-inch plywood to the size of the cushion. Apply spray adhesive to the beveled side of the foam and one side of the plywood (photo C), and then press them together (photo D).

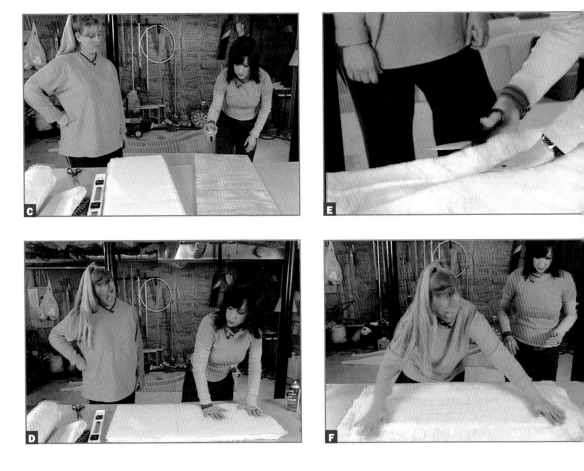

3 Cut batting to fit over the foam, with a few inches of extra material around all sides to overlap onto the backside of the plywood (photo E).

4 Apply spray adhesive to the foam and to the batting and then gently press them together (photo F).

5 Wrap muslin fabric over the batting (photo G) and around the back of the plywood, flipping the whole assembly over and holding the fabric tightly together on the back side.

6 Cut the muslin so that it overlaps the plywood by a few inches on all sides (photo H). Pull the muslin tight.

7 Starting in the middle of the seat, use a staple gun to fasten the muslin and batting to the back of the plywood (photo I). Work toward the corners, carefully pulling out all lumps and wrinkles as you go.

8 Fold the corners like "hospital corners" used when making a bed, and staple them in place.

9 Flatten any staples that don't sink fully by hitting them with a hammer (photo J).

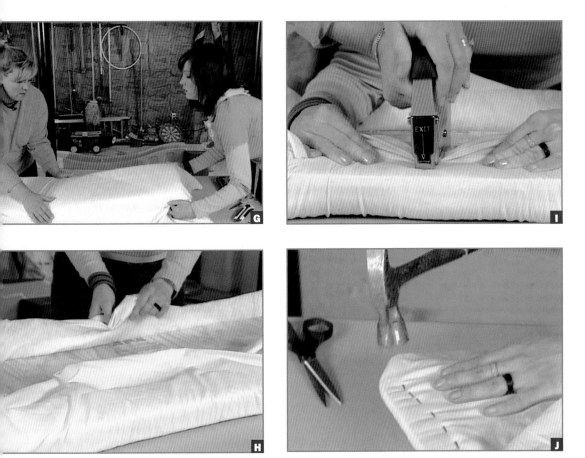

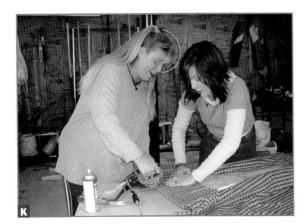

10 Repeat steps 18 through 22 with decorative fabric (photo K), being careful to smooth out the top as you work (photo L).

11 Use quick-lock clamps to position the seat over the lid (photo M) and then fasten it in place by inserting 1½-inch screws from the underside of the lid (photo N).

12 Cut a piece of 1-inch trim and fasten it to the exposed edge of the plywood lid using 1-inch finish nails (photo O).

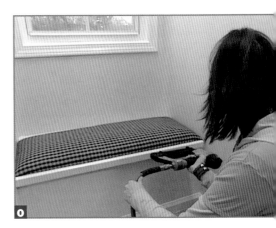

⬛ HANGING A WALLPAPER BORDER ⬛

You can buy pre-pasted borders at home centers. They're usually installed around the top edge of the wall, but for a baby or child's room, it's often better to hang the border closer to the midpoint of the wall, where the youngster will be able to see it.

You Will Need

Wallpaper border	Rags
4'- and/or 8'-level and pencil	Utility knife
Sharp scissors	Straightedge
5-gallon bucket	

1 Use a level to make a level pencil line all the way around the room (photo A) to mark the bottom edge of the border.

2 Working on one wall surface at a time, unroll the border, position it on the level line (photo B), and cut it to length using sharp scissors.

3 Gently fold the cut piece—without creasing it—to fit into a 5-gallon bucket filled with warm water, and submerge it for about 30 seconds (photo C). This activates the glue on the back of the paper.

4 Return the border piece to its intended location (photo D), carefully aligning it on the pencil line. Use a dry rag to press it against the wall, and, working from one end to the other, press air bubbles out (photo E).

5 Move to an adjacent section of wall and repeat the procedure. Carefully align the pattern from one piece to the next. Overlap the second piece over the first by about ¼ inch and then slice through both layers using a sharp utility knife against a straightedge. Then peel away the excess from each piece for a perfectly matched joint. Make sure seams fold at an internal corner or along a straight wall.

6 For external corners—that is, ones that jut into the room—continue the paper around the corner and onto the next wall without a seam.

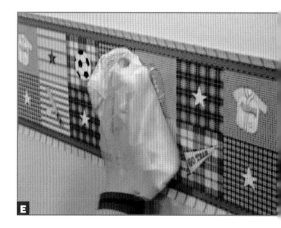

5

Living & Dining Rooms

Living and dining rooms are usually the most public spaces in a home. They also get a lot of traffic— from family and guests—so it's important these spaces be warm, inviting, and practical. When planning remodeling projects in these rooms, concentrate on a few specific areas, weigh your short- and long-term needs, and, if you have small children, consider their safety. Creativity also plays a major role in a successful remodel: Be sure to choose colors, lighting, and other decorative touches that will make you feel at home while conveying a sense of your family's personality and interests.

QUICK FIX

Kim and Phil's living room was vintage 1970's style, complete with textured walls and a metal sliding glass door that required two hands, and a lot of strength, to force open and shut. And then there was the mantelpiece with a faux-adobe look that came from a boxy wood frame coated with more textured plaster. Kim and Phil longed to update the space but didn't have the know-how to do it themselves.

◀ PROJECT SUMMARY ▶

Karl and Amy paid a visit to Kim and Phil's Las Vegas home and made quick work of transforming the room.

Smoothing Textured Walls. By scraping away some of the texture and then skimming over the walls with a few thin layers of drywall compound, the team was able to smooth out the finish.

Replacing a Mantel. Here's how to remove an ugly mantel and install something with plenty of character and charm.

Replacing a Sliding Glass Door. Whether you prefer new sliders or a set of French doors, replacing the existing unit is a fairly simple task, once you understand the procedure.

BEFORE: Intended to bring a south-western flare to the room, the chunky mantelpiece and textured walls only made the space look cheap—especially after Phil's earlier attempt at scraping down the walls, which left them gouged and scratched.

AFTER: Smooth walls, a mustard yellow paint job, and a custom wood mantelpiece have modernized and beautified the space.

SMOOTHING TEXTURED WALLS

Some textured walls contain asbestos, which can be released into the air if you scrape them, so don't attempt this process unless you're sure that the texture on your walls is asbestos-free.

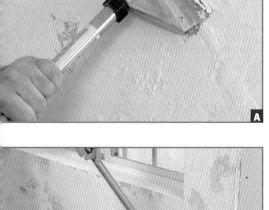

You Will Need

Dropcloths	Bucket
Floor scraper with 8" blade	Pre-mixed joint compound
Broom	Pre-mixed topping compound
Oil-based primer	10" taping trowel
Paintbrush	Rags
Paint roller and covers	Pole sander
Electric drill with mixer attachment	Fine-grit sandpaper

1 Empty the room of all furniture and belongings and lay down dropcloths before tackling this messy job.

2 Use a floor scraper with an 8-inch steel blade to scrape off the high spots on the wall (photo A). Because the blade is dull, it's less likely to dig into the work surface than a sharp wallpaper scraping blade would be.

3 Use a broom to brush loose debris and dust off of the wall surface (photo B).

4 Coat the surface with oil-based primer (photo C) to seal it and prepare it for drywall compound.

5 Use a power drill loaded with a mixer attachment (photo D) to combine equal parts of pre-mixed joint compound (designed for taping the joints between drywall boards) and pre-mixed topping compound (which is designed for skim coats on top of drywall).

6 Apply a thick layer of the mixture over the entire wall using a 10-inch trowel (photo E). Keep the trowel clean by wiping it with a rag occasionally, and use even strokes to create the flattest possible surface (photo F). If the trowel makes contact with the wall, you're pressing too hard.

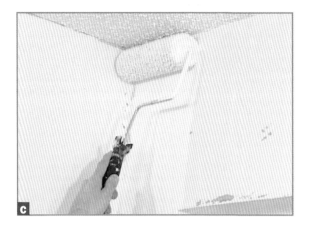

7 Once the compound has dried completely, sand it smooth using fine-grit sandpaper loaded into a pole sander.

8 Repeat steps 6 and 7 twice, and then a third time using only topping compound, which is thinner than joint compound. Keep the layer only 1 to 3 millimeters thick for this final coat. After a final sanding, the wall is ready for paint.

REPLACING A MANTEL

Many developers install cheap mantels as a way to cut the costs of constructing a home. Luckily, they're easy to replace, lending an instant upgrade to the fireplace—and the whole room. Whether your taste runs to the traditional or the contemporary, you can purchase stock or custom mantels in a host of different styles. Just make sure to follow your town's building code, which dictates the proper placement of combustible materials around the firebox.

You Will Need

- Utility knife
- Electronic stud finder with AC detection
- Flat bar
- Hammer
- Nippers
- Drywall
- 1⅝" drywall screws
- Drill/driver
- Fiberglass mesh tape
- Joint compound
- Taping trowel
- Taping knife
- Level
- Jigsaw
- Tape measure and pencil
- 3" drywall screws
- Construction adhesive

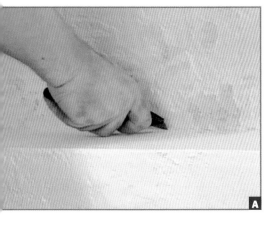

1 Score the seam where the old mantel meets the wall by cutting it with a sharp utility knife (photo A).

2 Use an electronic stud finder to locate the framing in the wall just above the mantel. It's a good idea to pick a stud finder that also will

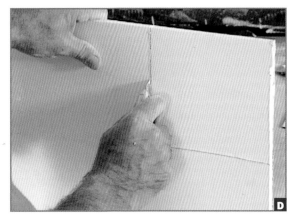

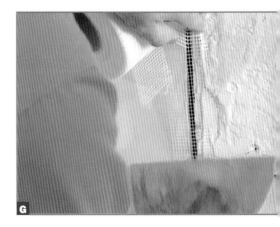

locate electrical wiring, just to confirm that there is none in the area where you're working.

3 Insert a flat bar between the mantel and the wall in the location of a stud. Hit the other end with a hammer, and then pry the old mantel away from the wall (photo B).

4 Repeat at the other stud locations across the top of the mantelpiece, gradually separating the mantel from the wall (photo C).

5 In this case, an old tile surround was also removed by prying against the backer-board underneath using the flat bar.

6 Remove any remaining nails or other debris from the exposed studs using nippers.

7 Patch the opening with drywall by using a utility knife to cut pieces to fit into the opening (photo D) and fastening them to the studs using 1⅝-inch drywall screws (photo E).

8 Insert additional screws around the perimeter of the existing drywall to ensure that it's firmly fastened to the studs (photo F).

9 Use fiberglass mesh tape (photo G) and joint compound to seal the seams around the new drywall, following the steps shown on pages 27-28.

10 Once the final coat of joint compound is dry, put the mantel into position (photo H), and test it for level (photo I). If necessary, trim one of the legs using a jig saw, so that the shelf is level.

11 To ensure plenty of solid material for fastening the mantel, many come with wood strips to install against the drywall. To do so, first use a pencil to lightly trace the outline of the mantel against the wall (photo J). Then measure the locations of the mating strips on the back of the mantel (photo K) and transfer those measurements to the wall. Fasten the wood strips to the wall using 3-inch drywall screws sunk into studs, apply a coat of construction adhesive to them, and position the mantel in place.

12 Install the mantel by sinking wood screws into the wall studs and the wood strips, using predrilled and countersunk holes (photo L).

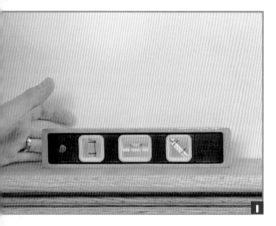

REPLACING A SLIDING GLASS DOOR

Thanks to years of exposure to the sun and rain, Kim and Phil's sliding glass door was nearly impossible to operate. So the *DIY to the Rescue* crew showed them how to tear it out and install a new French door that's made of insulated fiberglass with a maintenance-free aluminum exterior.

You Will Need

New French door	Caulk gun
Drill/driver	4' level
Flat bar	Wood shims
Hammer	Exterior trim
Pry bars	Manufacturer's door latch and locks
Reciprocating saw	Interior trim
Nippers	Miter saw
Broom	3" finish nails
Silicone caulk	2½" finish nails

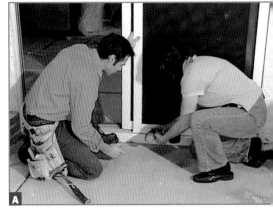

1 Remove the brackets that hold the sliding screen door at the top and bottom by backing out the screws (photo A). Then remove the screen door. Do the same process for the brackets that hold the two glass doors in their channels and lift those doors free (photo B).

2 Use a flat bar and hammer to pry off the interior and exterior molding around the door opening (photo C).

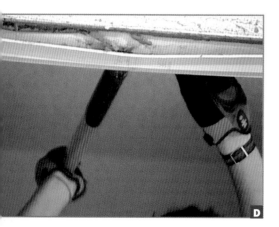

3 Back out the screws that secure the door jamb to the framing in the walls.

4 Use pry bars to pull the door jamb away from the walls (photo D). It may be necessary to cut the jamb using a reciprocating saw (photo E).

5 Once the jamb is removed, check the framing around the opening for nails and debris and pull them off using nippers. Sweep the floor (photo F).

6 Test fit the door (photo G) to make sure that it fits in the opening, and then remove it again.

7 Apply a thick bead of silicone caulk on the flange on the exterior perimeter of the door (photo H) and three rows of caulk on the base of the opening where the door will sit (photo I). This will create a watertight seal around the door.

8 Lift the door into position again. Check the door for level, plumb, and square, and use shims as necessary to adjust its position. Once the door is placed perfectly, fasten it in by inserting screws through the predrilled holes in the flange and into the wall studs (photo J).

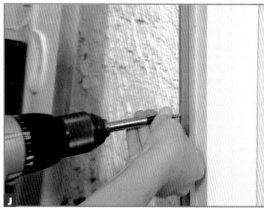

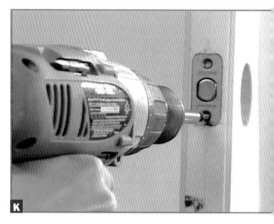

9 Assemble and attach the exterior trim. In this case, it came as part of the door kit; it is made of aluminum, and simply snaps into place on the edge of the door frame.

10 Attach the door latch and lock sets into predrilled holes by following the manufacturer's instructions (photo K).

11 Use a miter saw to cut interior molding to fit the opening. You can put 45-degree angles on the corners or use corner blocks, which add a decorative touch and mean only 90-degree cuts will be needed (photo L).

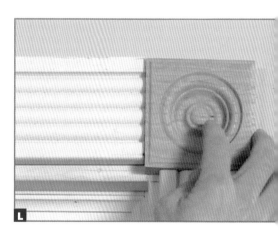

12 Attach the interior trim to the wall studs using 3-inch finish nails and the door jamb using 2½-inch finish nails.

PATCH WORK

The worst problem in Stephanie and Craig's living room was that the original builder never installed a hearth, so the fireplace didn't meet code and wasn't safe to use. Solving that problem required the expertise of a mason, but the homeowners were able to resolve two smaller and more common dilemmas themselves, with the help of the *DIY to the Rescue* team.

◀ PROJECT SUMMARY ▶

The DIY portions of this rescue addressed two very common household woes—one underfoot and the other overhead.

Repairing Hardwood Floors. A one-time leak in the previous sliding glass doors had warped, stained, and rotted a few floorboards, so Amy showed Stephanie how to replace them.

Patching Drywall. Amy also gave Craig a lesson in creating a drywall patch, even when there's nothing behind the hole on which to fasten the drywall.

Before: In addition to a fireplace that needs a hearth in order to meet fire code, the living room needs two DIY patch-up jobs—for some rotted floor boards and a hole in the drywall ceiling.

After: Masons have constructed a new hearth and, with the help of Amy and Karl, Stephanie, and Craig have installed new floorboards and drywall.

HARDWOOD FLOOR REPAIR

There are all sorts of reasons that you might have to patch your hardwood floors, from leaks to reconfigured floor plans to general wear and tear. And in any of these situations, you'll need to piece in new flooring boards—and give them a finish that matches the rest of the floor.

You Will Need

Hammer	Replacement flooring
Wood chisel	Miter saw
Drill/driver	Flooring nails
1" spade bit	Nail set
Flat bar	Pneumatic nail gun
Nippers	Random orbit sander
Stiff brush	Heavy, medium, fine grit sandpaper
Heavy-duty vacuum	Wood stain
Tar paper	Rag
Utility knife	Colored wood putty
Staple gun or staple hammer	Water-based polyurethane
Tape measure	Foam paint brush

1 Remove the damaged boards by breaking out material from one of them using a hammer and wood chisel—or a drill loaded with a 1-inch spade bit. Then, work a flat bar into the hole and pry out that board and any others that need replacement (photo A). Make sure not to break the tongue or groove on the edge of the adjacent boards that aren't removed.

2 Use nippers and a stiff brush to remove any nails and wood scraps left from the damaged boards.

3 Clean the area thoroughly with a heavy duty vacuum (photo B).

4 Use a utility knife to cut tar paper to fit the opening and install it with staples loaded into a staple gun (photo C) or staple hammer. Use a regular hammer to flatten any staples that aren't fully sunk into the subfloor.

5 You can purchase new tongue-and-groove flooring at any lumber yard or home center. Bring one of the old pieces along when you go and ask the salesperson to match the wood species. That will help the repair blend in with the old floor.

6 Measure for the first piece of replacement flooring, remembering to tuck the tape measure under any existing baseboard (photo D). Also, subtract ¼ inch from the total length of the board to allow for expansion and contraction of the wood.

7 Transfer the measurement to a replacement board, orienting it so that a factory tongue or groove is on the end (photo E) to mate with the end of the board it will butt against. Also ensure that the main tongue and groove are oriented properly for the existing floor.

8 Use a miter saw to cut the first piece of replacement flooring (photo F) to size.

9 Lay the board so that either tongue slides into the existing floorboard's groove or vice versa. Press it firmly against the neighboring boards. If the board is against a wall, position the ¼-inch expansion space to hide under the baseboard at the end.

10 If possible, nail the board in place with flooring nails at a 45-degree angle right in the corner where the tongue begins. If this isn't possible, you'll have to face nail, which means nailing though the top of the board (photo G). You can use a hammer and nail set, but a pneumatic nail gun will reduce the chances of marring the wood surface.

E

F

G

TIPS | DIY Network Home Improvement

RESOURCEFUL PATCHING

If your repair is small, carefully remove a few boards from a closet or an attic landing to use as patching material. These boards will match the original floor much better than new pieces will—and they might even have the same finish on them. Then you can simply patch the closet or attic landing with new material, since a perfect match is a lot less important there.

11 Continue cutting and installing boards, allowing a ¼-inch expansion space on the end of each row and always staggering the seams so they're less noticeable.

12 Unless you've used perfectly matched boards from a closet or attic or basement landing (see Tip, below), the next step is to sand the new boards down to match the surface of the old ones (photo H). Use a random orbit sander and a succession of heavy, then medium, then fine grit sandpaper.

13 Bring one of the damaged boards to a paint shop to select a few stains that look like close matches. Then use a rag to apply a test sample of each stain on some scraps of the new flooring material. Make sure to keep track of which stain you use on each sample, how many coats of stain you apply, and how long you leave the stain in place. (Staining involves wiping on the stain and then wiping it off again. The longer you wait to wipe it off, the darker the results will be. You'll need notes from your test samples to be able to duplicate your results, or to adjust the timing for a lighter or darker finish.)

14 Once the stain samples have dried, compare them to the floor. If you have a perfect match, you're ready to stain the repair. If not, try adjusting the timing, combining two of the stain products, or purchasing different stain products and testing again.

15 Apply the stain to the new flooring using a rag and long, even strokes (photo I) and being careful to follow the exact procedure that you recorded on the winning test sample.

16 Once the stain has dried, fill the nail holes (if you face nailed) with colored wood putty in the closest possible shade, and allow it to dry.

17 Apply three coats of water-based polyurethane by brushing on each coat, allowing it to dry thoroughly, and sanding lightly with fine-grit sandpaper between coats. A matte finish urethane often works best for matching an old finish.

DRYWALL PATCH

Stephanie and Craig also had a small hole in the ceiling drywall from an old range hood that had been removed. They had tried putting a piece of drywall into the hole, but because there was nothing to nail it to, they needed Amy's help.

You Will Need

Scrap wood	Utility knife
1¼" drywall screws	Drywall rasp
Drill/driver	Fiberglass mesh tape
Tape measure and pencil	Joint compound
Drywall	Taping knife
Combination or T-square	Fine-grit sanding block

1 Cut a piece of scrap wood a few inches longer than the hole. Insert it into the hole and position it so to cover the opening and overlap one full side (photo A).

2 Use a drill/driver to sink 1¼-inch drywall screws through the existing drywall around the perimeter of the hole and into the scrap wood.

3 Unless the board covers the entire hole, cut an additional scrap to cover the opposite side and install it the same way.

4 Measure the dimensions of the hole (photo B), and transfer the measurements to a piece of drywall using a combination square or T-square (photo C). Cut the drywall by scoring the paper with a utility knife, breaking the board along that line (photo D), and then cutting the paper on the other side.

5 Test fit the patch in the hole. If it's a little oversized, shave it down with a drywall rasp.

6 Once you have a good fit, use the utility knife or rasp to cut a 45-degree bevel around the entire perimeter (photo E).

7 Bevel the edges of the existing drywall around the hole as well (photo F). This creates a V-groove that will simplify the taping process.

B

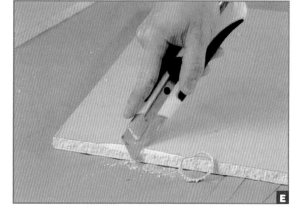

E

D

F

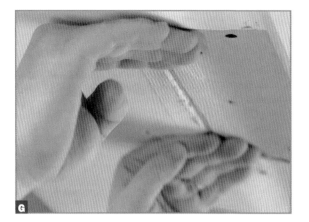

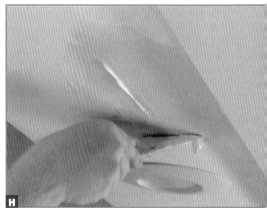

8 Fasten the patch to the wood backing using 1¼-inch drywall screws and the drill/driver.

9 Press fiberglass mesh drywall tape over all of the seams (photo G) and use a taping knife to apply a thin layer of joint compound to the seams and screw holes (photo H).

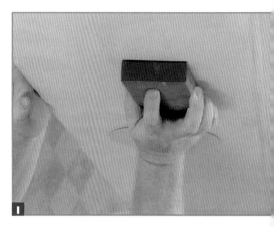

10 Allow the compound to dry completely, and then sand with a fine-grit sanding block (photo I).

11 Apply another thin coat of joint compound, using the taping knife to feather out the edges and to smooth away ridges and bumps (photo J).

12 Sand, apply a third coat, and give it a final sanding. Then, the patch is ready for paint.

DINING ROOM DRESS UP

Homeowners Tara and Donovan loved to host dinner parties, but they hated their dining room. The doors and drawers on its corner china cabinet were drooping and inoperable. The room's original wainscot was cracked and caked with a century of built-up paint, and its window overlooked their messy office and exercise room. Plus, the room's only light fixture was a 1970's ceiling fan.

Before: The doors and drawers in the corner cupboard no longer worked and the whole unit looked dated.

After: The revamped corner cupboard still feels at home in the century-old house, but it has been totally restored— and updated with a modern color and hardware.

PROJECT SUMMARY

The crew resolved the dining room problems with four great projects that handy homeowners can put to use in their own houses.

Restoring a Built-In Cabinet. An old corner cupboard or butler's pantry can be a wonderful period feature, as long as it looks good and works well. Here's how to rejuvenate yours.

Laying Glass Block. Want plenty of light without any view? Looking for a unique and stylish focal point for the space? Replacing a problem window with glass block can turn a flaw into an asset.

Building Traditional Wainscot. Real beadboard is a bit more time consuming to install than faux beadboard paneling, described on pages 118-121, but the look of true beadboard is more authentic.

Installing a New Ceiling Fixture. Tara and Donovan replaced their old oak ceiling fan with a contemporary, brushed-chrome, pendant light, and you can follow the same steps for replacing any light fixture.

Before: A previous owner had actually painted the lower sash of the window to block the views out to the porch.

After: The new glass block window brings an architectural feel to the space.

A

B

RESTORING A BUILT-IN CABINET

Whether it's a corner cupboard like this one, a wall unit, or a buffet, any built-in dining room cabinet can be a convenient and attractive place to store china and other serving ware. But the ravages of time, heavy use, or overzealous painters can dilapidate and render cupboards nonfunctional. Here's how to refurbish a failing built-in.

You Will Need

Screwdriver set	1½" paneling nails
Drill/driver	Electronic stud finder
Reciprocating saw	1x2 board
Hammer	2" finish nails
Flat bar	Nail set
Tape measure	Screws
½" birch plywood	Quick-lock clamps
Table saw	Tape measure
Decorative molding	¾" birch plywood
Miter saw	Paint and brushes
1" finish nails	Hinges
Pneumatic nail gun (optional)	Knobs and pulls
Circular saw	1' level
Luaun plywood	

C

D

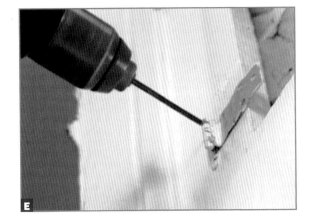

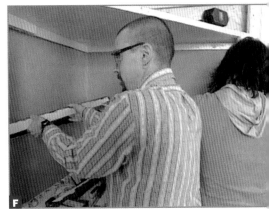

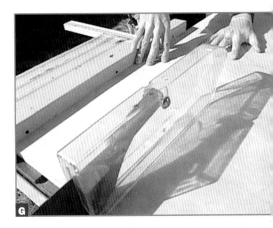

1 Begin by removing all of the drawers, and then backing out the hinge screws to remove the doors (photo A).

2 It's simplest to replace poorly functioning drawers with cabinets, so use a reciprocating saw to slice through the center of the shelves (photo B) as well as the old frames separating the drawer openings (photo C). Then, use a hammer and flat bar to pop out the cut shelves (photo D).

3 Use a screwdriver or drill/driver to back out the screws from any remaining hardware (photo E), and use a flat bar and hammer to remove the shelf-support cleats from the interior walls of the cupboard (photo F).

4 Order new doors from a cabinet shop, or make your own from ½-inch birch plywood, as follows.

5 Take door measurements from the old doors or the cabinet and transfer them to the plywood. Cut the doors to size using a table saw (photo G). Make sure to orient the plywood grain vertically when planning the cuts.

6 To frame the face of each door with decorative molding, such as the flat ½x1-inch strips used for the 5 wicks, cut the trim on a miter saw with 45-degree angles at each corner. Old glass-paned doors should be reused if possible, since they're much more difficult to build from scratch. If the glass is broken, bring the entire door to a glass shop for reglazing.

7 Fasten the trim to the door with 1-inch finish nails, using a hammer and nail set or a pneumatic nail gun (photo H).

8 Use a circular saw to cut ¼-inch luaun plywood to fit the back walls of the cabinet with the grain running vertically.

9 Position each back section in place (photo I), check the fit, and fasten it. In this case, the old walls are wood, so the new luaun was nailed with a pneumatic brad nailer (photo J) with no need to search for studs. If your walls are plaster or drywall, use a electronic stud finder and nail to the studs using 1½-inch paneling nails.

10 Cut new shelf cleats from a 1x2 board, tack them in place with 2-inch finish nails, and then use screws to fasten them to the wall studs or underlying plywood after predrilling and countersinking the holes.

11 Measure and then use a circular saw against a clamped straightedge to cut new shelves from ¾-inch birch plywood (photo K). To learn how to set up a straightedge, see pages 49-50, steps 8-9.

12 Test fit the shelves and make any necessary adjustments. Then remove them, and paint everything before putting them back. That will simplify the painting task.

13 Attach the new doors using the hinges of your choice, and fasten new knobs and pulls to the doors as well (photo L).

LAYING GLASS BLOCK

Because their dining room window looks out on a messy unfinished porch that they use as an office and exercise room, Tara and Donovan wanted to replace it with something that would let in light without letting guests see out. So the *DIY to the Rescue* team suggested filling the opening with glass block, an eye-catching feature that also provides plenty of insulation. Here's how the job is done:

You Will Need

Flat bar	Glass block plastic channel
Drill/driver	Brads
Screwdriver set	White paint
Utility knife	Glass block spacers
Hammer and nail set	Level
Reciprocating saw	Wood shims
Tape measure	Trim boards
Glass block	Finish nails
1x4 pine	Pneumatic nail gun (optional)
Miter Saw	Glass block caulk
1½" wood screws or nails	

1 To take out the old window, remove the stop, which is the strip of wood that's attached to the jamb to hold the lower sash in place. If it's fastened with nails, pry it loose with a flat bar (photo A). Or if it's attached with screws, simply back those out to free the stop.

2 With the stops removed from the sides and top of the opening, lift out the lower sash. If it has been painted shut, you'll need to cut the old paint with a utility knife and possibly use the flat bar to help remove the sash (photo B). Use the claw of your hammer or a flat bar to disconnect the old sash cords from the sash, if necessary.

A

B

TIPS | DIY Network Home Improvement

GLASS BLOCK OPTION

For large openings, where the weight of glass block might be too much for the support structure, consider acrylic block, which is less heavy than glass.

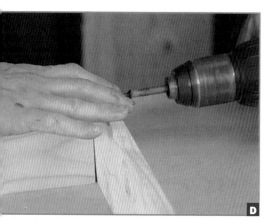

3 Next, use the flat bar to remove the parting stop, which is another strip of wood attached to the jamb, in this case between the two sashes.

4 That will enable you to remove the upper sash. Again, you may need to disconnect the old sash cords from the sash when you pull it free.

5 Remove any old weight pulleys (photo C) or other hardware by backing out the screws.

6 Use the flat bar and hammer to remove all trim and jambs. (It may help to cut the jambs first with a reciprocating saw.)

7 Measure the rough opening of the window and take those measurements to your home center or glass shop. Choose the size and style of block that best works with your opening. The store can help you make your choices and tell you what installation parts you will need.

8 Follow the instructions that come with the glass block to determine the dimensions for a simple wood frame made of 1x4 pine. Then cut the pieces on a miter saw and attach the bottom to the sides using 1½-inch screws (photo D).

9 Install a temporary brace at the top of the frame to hold the sides at the right opening size (photo E).

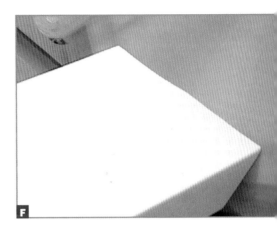

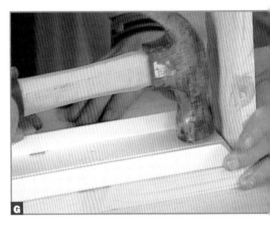

10 Cut the plastic channel sold with the block to fit inside the wood frame. Using the miter saw, cut 45 degree angles at the corners (photo F).

11 Use the brads sold with the product to attach the bottom and side channels to the wood frame (photo G).

12 Fasten the remaining piece of channel to the remaining piece of 1x4 using the brads.

13 Touch up the brad heads with paint (photo H) so that you won't see them through the glass.

14 Lay the blocks into the channel, using the provided spacers to separate each block from its neighbor (photo I).

15 Once two rows are in place, stand the unit on end, and continue laying the blocks. Use a hammer to tap spacers between them after each row is assembled, and then lay long spacers over the top of the row (photo J).

16 Add additional braces to the frame as you work to keep the sides from opening up and letting the blocks spill out (photo K).

17 Lay the remaining piece of frame and channel in place and fasten with 1½-inch wood screws or nails (photo L).

18 Lift the assembly into the window opening (photo M).

19 Check it for level and plumb and adjust as necessary with wood shims. Then, toenail or toescrew the frame into the adjacent wall studs.

20 Remove the temporary braces by backing out the screws (photo N).

21 Measure the window and then cut new trim boards to surround it, using 45-degree angles cut on the miter saw.

22 Fasten the trim in place using finish nails and a hammer and nail set, or a pneumatic nail gun.

23 Apply clear glass block caulk to all of the joints between the blocks and around the their entire perimeter (photo O).

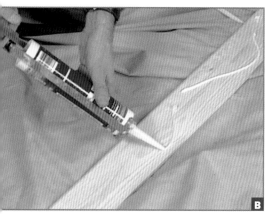

BUILDING TRADITIONAL WAINSCOT

Tara chose beadboard wainscot for the dining room because it feels both traditional (which is her taste) and contemporary (which is Donovan's preference). Plus, it will protect the walls from getting dented by the dining room chairs. You can find a quicker process for this job on pages 118-121 using beadboard paneling, but the process shown here uses real beadboard, which has deeper and more authentic detailing.

You Will Need

- ½" finish-grade plywood or ⅜" rough plywood
- Electronic stud finder
- 1¾" screws
- ½" thick beadboard
- Miter saw
- Caulk gun
- Construction adhesive
- 2' level
- 1" finish nails
- Tape measure and pencil
- Pneumatic nail gun
- Jigsaw
- Hammer and nailset (optional)
- Baseboard
- 1½" finish nails
- Chair rail
- Wood putty
- Painter's caulk
- Electrical box extenders
- Cover plates

1 Choose the height for your wainscot. There are no rules about this, though it's a good idea to make it at least as high as the backs of your dining room chairs. Tara chose 38 inches for hers. Remove all hardware and trim from the walls below that point. Also, turn off electricity to the room, remove any outlet face plates, and remove outlet receptacles from their boxes, allowing them to dangle freely during the work.

2 Because the old walls in this house were so severely damaged, the crew gutted the walls and installed ½-inch finish-grade plywood over the studs (photo A). If that's not the case in your situation, add ⅜-inch plywood over the existing walls at the height of the wainscot using 1¾-inch screws sunk into studs located with an electronic stud finder—or consider using beadboard paneling instead of individual boards (see pages 118-121).

3 Using a miter saw, cut the first ½-inch beadboard to length. Use a caulk gun to apply a zigzag of construction adhesive to the back side (photo B), and position it at the far edge of the wall.

4 Use a 2-foot level to ensure that it's plumb (photo C). Getting this first piece perfect will help to ensure that all of the others line up perfectly vertical as well.

5 Nail it into the plywood backing using 1-inch finish nails. You can use a hammer and nail set, but a pneumatic nail gun will work much faster—and reduce the chances of marring the surface with an errant hammer blow (photo D).

6 Set a level (the longer the better) on top of the first board and use it to transfer a level line around the room (photo E).

7 Check the distances from the floor to ceiling every few feet and see whether they vary. If not, you can cut numerous boards to the length of the first one, assembly-line style, by setting the stop on your miter saw to that length. If heights vary, measure each piece as you go.

8 Apply construction adhesive to each board, lay it in place, and nail it. Use a jigsaw to notch boards for windows and outlet boxes as necessary (photo F).

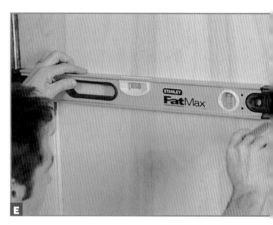

9 Once all of the beadboard is installed, cut baseboard to length and fasten it to the beadboard using 1½-inch finish nails, creating coped joints at the ends. (See pages 142-143 for more about cutting trim.)

10 Do the same for chair rail molding at the top of the beadboard, but fasten it either to the plywood wall backing or to the studs.

11 Fill all nail holes with putty, and caulk all seams. Then, paint the wainscot. Reattach the electrical outlets to their boxes, using box extenders if necessary, and attach new cover plates.

INSTALLING A NEW CEILING FIXTURE

Swapping out a dated chandelier, ceiling fan, or any light fixture for something more to your liking is one of the quickest and most affordable ways to upgrade the feeling of an entire space.

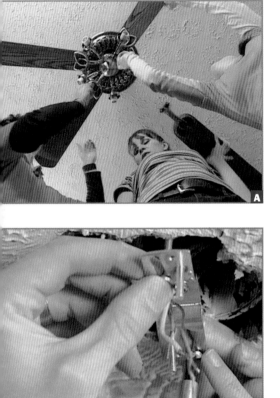

You Will Need

Ladder	Needle-nose pliers
Screwdriver set	Light fixture
Wire nuts	

1 Turn off the power to the light by flipping the circuit breaker or removing the fuse. Then double check that the light is indeed inoperable.

2 Remove the old light fixture—or, in this case, the ceiling fan—by disassembling it (photo A).

3 Loosen the wire nuts from the fixture's base and remove it.

4 Attach the new fixture's bracket to the existing electrical box (photo B).

5 Connect the fixture's white wire to the house's white wire by twisting the ends together in a clockwise motion and then twisting a wire nut over them so that the uncoated tips are completely covered (photo C).

6 Connect the black wires following the same procedure.

7 Connect the copper wire to the green nut on the electrical box.

8 If you see something different in your electrical box than is described here, or are unsure about any connection, stop and call an electrician for help. Many have 24-hour emergency services that will come quickly.

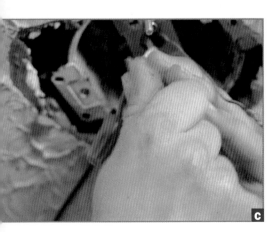

9 Gently tuck the wiring into the box and lift the fixture into place (photo D).

10 Attach the fixture to the mounting plate using the provided hardware (photo E).

11 Screw in a light bulb, and turn on the power.

TILE STYLE

When homeowner Melissa tore out the ugly, wall-to-wall carpet in her dining room, she didn't uncover hardwood floors hiding underneath. She found grungy peel-and-stick vinyl tiles. And to make matters worse, the tackless strip that had held the carpet around the perimeter of the room had torn and shredded the vinyl. She could see a rough plywood subfloor through those holes, so pulling up the vinyl wasn't the solution. Instead, she began thinking of what she could lay on top of the old flooring.

PROJECT SUMMARY

A new ceramic tile floor transformed Melissa's dining room, along with fresh moldings and paint.

Laying a Ceramic Tile Floor. The team laid a new large-format ceramic tile floor that not only lends sophistication to the room but the visual impact of the grid helps to make it feel bigger too.

BEFORE: The vinyl floor in Melissa's dining room was peeling up in spots.

AFTER: New ceramic floor tiles, new trim, and new paint have dressed up the room.

You Will Need

Flat bar	Straightedge	Grout float
Hammer	Plastic tile spacers	Sponges
Broom	Snap tile cutter	Lint-free towels
Vacuum	Wet saw with diamond-tip blade	Baseboard
Tape measure	Thinset mortar	Shoe molding
Concrete backerboard	Electric drill	Miter saw
Chalk line	Paddle mixer attachment	Coping saw
Backerboard nails	5-gallon bucket	3" finish nails
Carbide-tipped scoring tool	Gloves	Electronic stud finder
Angle grinder with masonry blade	Notched trowel	Thresholds
Ceramic floor tiles	Grout	Ring shank nails

A

B

LAYING A CERAMIC TILE FLOOR

Melissa chose a faux-stone floor tile that's environmentally friendly because it's made from recycled glass and clay materials. But the following installation procedure is appropriate for any ceramic floor tile, and is designed for installation over a wood subfloor.

1 Use a flat bar and hammer to remove the baseboards, and then clean the floor thoroughly with a broom and vacuum.

2 To create a flat, smooth, and stable subfloor for the tile, you'll need to lay down concrete backerboard. Measure out $36\frac{1}{8}$ inches at each end of the room's longest wall and snap a chalk line between the two marks (photo A). This will be your guideline for the first row of 3x5-foot backerboard (with a $\frac{1}{8}$-inch allowance for expansion).

3 Align the first backerboard along the chalk mark and fasten it through the old vinyl floor and into the wood subfloor underneath. Use the nails recommended by the manufacturer, set every 6 inches or so across the sheet.

4 Lay down another sheet end-to-end with the first, and nail it in place, leaving a $\frac{1}{8}$-inch gap between the boards—and around all boards—to allow for expansion. To cut the backerboard, score it a few times with a carbide-tipped blade (photo B), and then lift it in the direction of the cut to snap it (photo C). For notches and complex cuts, use an angle grinder.

5 For each successive row, stagger the joints by 16 inches or more to reduce the chances of tiles cracking from movement between the backerboard sheets.

6 Once the backerboard layer is complete, choose a starting point for your floor tiles. This should be the most visible spot on the floor, since the tiles here will be installed whole. Tiles along the room's other walls are likely to be cut. For this project, Karl began at the doorway, where most people will enter the room.

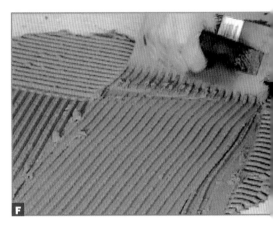

7 Lay out the entire floor with tiles, using a straightedge to help align them and plastic spacers to ensure that they're spaced evenly. Consider whether adjusting the spacing could eliminate some cutting, and readjust using spacers of a different width if necessary.

9 Cut the tiles as needed. For straight cuts, use a snap tile cutter, which scores the tile so you can break it along the line. For notches, use a wet saw, which has an industrial, diamond-tipped blade and a pump that keeps it wet, to cool the blade as it's cutting through the tile (photo D).

10 Once the entire floor is laid out, pick up the tiles and stack them in orderly piles so you know exactly where each cut one belongs.

11 Mix a batch of thinset mortar using a 5-gallon bucket and an electric drill loaded with a paddle mixing attachment (photo E). Follow the thinset manufacturer's instructions for mixing.

12 Use a notched trowel to spread the thinset onto the backboard, making sure to create an even layer over about a four-square-foot area (photo F). Work quickly because the mortar will begin setting in about 30 minutes (photo G).

13 Lay the first four tiles in position (photo H) and insert spacers into the gaps between them (photo I). This will keep all of the joints equal and help to level the height of all the tiles as well. Press the tiles firmly into the thinset for a good bond and to ensure a flat surface, even if the subfloor is a little bit uneven.

TIPS | DIY Network
Home Improvement

CORNERED!

**Always work toward a doorway, so
you don't tile yourself into a corner.**

14 Repeat steps 12 and 13 for sets of two to four tiles at a time until the floor is completely covered with tiles (photo J). Do not step on the tiles until the mortar has cured overnight. Once the mortar has cured, remove the spacers.

15 Use the paddle mixer and 5-gallon bucket to mix a batch of grout in the color of your choice.

16 Scoop up some mortar onto a grout float and lay it over the joints between the tiles (photo K), being careful to completely fill every crevice with grout. Hold the float at about a 30-degree angle to apply the grout and about a 45-degree angle to wipe away the excess. Work diagonally across the joints to avoid

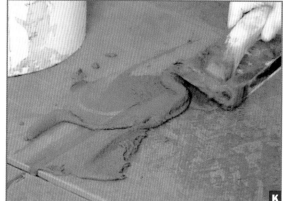

gouging out the grout as you cross them. Wipe excess grout off the float frequently using a towel.

17 Once all of the joints are grouted, use a sponge dipped in clean water to wipe the surface of the tiles to remove excess grout (photo L). Allow the grout to cure for a few hours. Use lint-free towels to buff the surface of the tile and remove the remaining film of grout (photo M). Allow the grout to cure a few more hours, and buff again, if necessary.

18 Install new baseboard and shoe molding by mitering the exterior corners and coping the interior ones (these processes are described on pages 142-143) and installing them with 3-inch finish nails. Sink the nails into wall studs, which can be found with an electronic stud finder.

19 Cut wood thresholds to cover the joint between the tiles and adjacent flooring, then nail the thresholds down with ring shank nails.

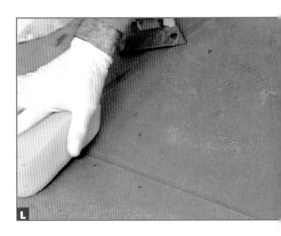

L

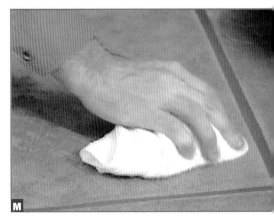

M

DIY to the Rescue

6

Entryways

Believe in making a good first impression? Then it may be time to fix up the entryway to your home. Too often our foyers and hallways are drab and utilitarian—a coat rack or pegs on the wall and an uninspired carpet on the floor. These spaces can be both practical and stylish, though, and you can easily add a lot of personality with a few weekend projects. Install bright new flooring, paint or panel the walls, or add some stylish storage or decorator lighting.

RE-MAKING AN ENTRANCE

Homeowner DeeAnn is a very capable do-it-yourselfer, but even her best efforts couldn't resolve the problems with her cavernous entry hall. She had given the two-story foyer a fresh paint job using sanded paint in order to bring color and texture to the high walls, but the room still felt oversized and vacant. And the dark stain that she had put on the wood floors wound up exaggerating the height of the light ceilings. Plus, the floor stain was missing in one spot, where she had been unable to move a large armoire that she and husband Bill have since gotten rid of.

Before: A dark brown floor and sand-painted walls didn't make the Bowers' foyer seem cozy.

After: Eye-catching wall panels and a new vinyl laminate floor have transformed the space, brightening it and giving it a sophisticated look.

PROJECT SUMMARY

The *DIY to the Rescue* crew's answer to DeeAnn's foyer problems was two-fold.

Installing Wall Panels. By subdividing the walls with plywood squares framed with moldings, the team broke-up the walls visually, helping to reduce their too-tall feel.

Laying Vinyl Strip Flooring. These strips are cut with shears, installed with glue, and impervious to the water and grime of an entry hall.
Yet they look just like real wood.

INSTALLING WALL PANELS

This process is a bit more involved than installing sheets of prefab paneling or even strips of beadboard, but the results are well worth the extra effort. The look of the framed panels is a very authentic traditional design that brings visual appeal to the room and reduces the need for any artwork or other decoration in the space.

You Will Need

Screwdriver set	Chair rail
Utility knife	Door and window casing
Hammer	Baseboard
Flat bar	Shoe molding
Rotary sander with vacuum attachment	4' level
Dust masks	Framing square
Safety goggles	Table saw or circular saw
Laser level	Construction adhesive
Tape measure and pencil	Finish nails
Chalk line	Nailset
Ladders or scaffolding	Pneumatic nail gun (optional)
Paintbrushes	Miter saw
Rollers and roller covers	Coping saw
Paint trays	Speed square
Primer	Painter's caulk
Paint	Caulk gun
⅜" birch plywood	Wood putty
Capping rail	

1 Begin by removing all light fixtures (photo A), as well as the switch and outlet covers (photo B), by backing out the screws.

2 Use a sharp utility knife to score the paint around the door and window casings, baseboards, and any other moldings (photo C), and then use a hammer and flat bar to remove them from the walls (photo D).

3 To remove the sand paint from the Bowers' walls, the crew used a rotary sander attached to a high-filtration vacuum (photo E). This eliminates much of the dust, but safety goggles and a dust mask are still essential gear for the job. (Sanding is only necessary if the walls are textured.)

4 Because this is a two-story foyer, the crew decided to panel the lower half only. To do so, they established the dividing line at the height of the upstairs floor and transferred it around the room by holding a laser level in place on each wall (photo F), making pencil marks at each end of its line, and then snapping chalk lines to connect the marks (photo G).

5 Use rollers and brushes to paint the lower portion of the walls one color and the upper portion another (photo H). You'll need ladders and scaffolding to reach the highest points in a two-story foyer like this one. Stay at least an inch away from the chalk line when rolling to be sure you don't mix chalk into the paint, and then carefully paint along that line with a brush—but don't worry about creating an exact line because the transition will be covered with a piece of wood molding later.

6 Also, prime and paint ⅜-inch birch plywood (photo I), as well as capping rails that will frame each panel, the chair rail, new door and window casings, the baseboard, and the shoe molding.

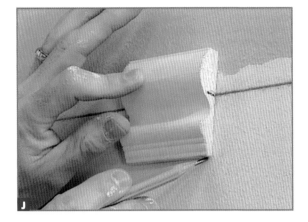

7 Three segments of paneling will cover the lower paint color, and your next step is to determine the height of each segment. To do so, you'll need to make three marks on the wall.

8 Hold a piece of chair rail molding in place over the color transition at the top and make a mark at the bottom of the molding (photo J) and then measure down 4 inches and make an additional mark (photo K).

9 Use a 4-foot level to transfer the height of the door opening to the location of the mark you made in the previous step. Make an additional mark 4 inches above the door-height mark as well (photo L).

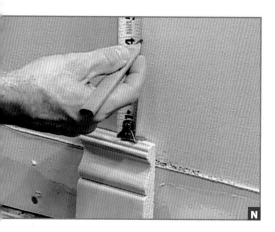

10 Place a scrap of baseboard into position, and make a mark 4 inches above its top (photo M).

11 Measure between the mark above the baseboard and the one that's at the height of the door opening (photo N). Two panels will be placed between these marks, with a 4-inch space between them, so subtract 4 inches from the total measurement. Divide the result in half for the height of the lower two panels. The third panel will be sized to fit between the line 4 inches below the chair rail and the one 4 inches above the door opening. Make all of those marks on the wall.

12 To transfer the marks around the room, you could use a level, but a storyboard is a better way. This is simply a piece of scrap wood on which you transfer all of the markings to serve as a template that you can move around the room (photo O).

13 Use the storyboard to mark the panel heights every 16 inches or so all the way around the room (photo P).

14 To determine the width of your panels, simply divide each wall section into equal parts, remembering to account for the 4-inch spacing between all panels (photo Q).

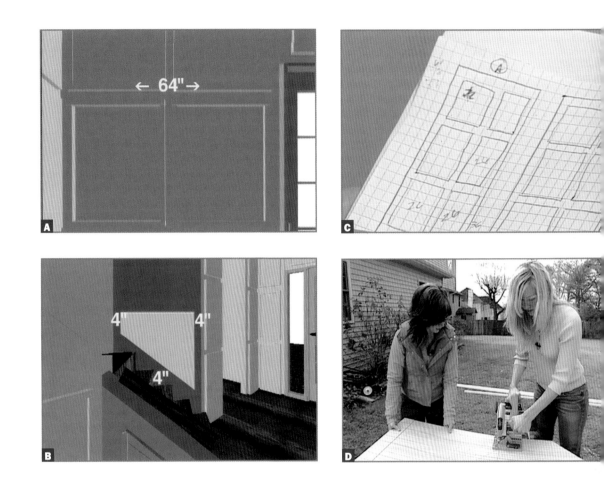

INSTALLING WALL PANELS

1 Once all of the panel-width markings have been added to the walls, use a 4-foot level to draw on the wall the exact size and placement of each panel (photo A).

2 For the panel above the stairs, keep the top aligned with its neighbors in the rest of the room, and create the angle for the bottom of the panel by measuring 4 inches off the stairway stringer at each end and snapping a chalk line (photo B).

3 Make rough sketches of the panel layout. Measure the exact size needed for each piece, and note the sizes on the sketch so you can keep track of where each one goes (photo C).

4 Use a tape measure and framing square to draw out each panel on the back of the birch plywood, and use a table saw or circular saw to make the cuts (photo D, previous page). Working from the back will help to protect the freshly painted surfaces, and undersizing the panels by ⅛- to ¼-inch will ensure that they fit. (The trim you'll install later will cover any gaps.)

5 To install the first panel, draw an X on the back of the panel with a thin bead of construction adhesive (photo E). Set the panel into place on the lines drawn for it (photo F).

6 Use finish nails to attach the panel to the drywall. There's no need to hit the studs because the nails only anchor the panel while the construction adhesive dries. Angle the nails slightly so that they'll provide a good hold (photo G) and locate them near the edge so the heads will be covered by trim later. You can use a hammer and nail set or a pneumatic nail gun, which will greatly simplify this job and reduce the chances of marring the surface.

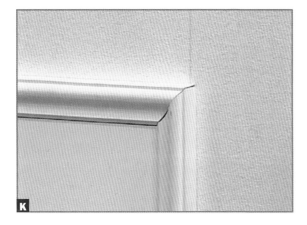

7 Repeat steps 5 and 6 for each panel (photo H).

8 The capping rail has a "rebate" in the back that's designed to sit over the edge of the panel (photo I). Use the measurements on the rough sketches for sizing the trim, and use a miter saw to create 45-degree angles on all of the ends (photo J). For the angled panels along the stairs, you'll need to use a speed square to determine the total angle of each corner, then divide that number in half, and set the miter saw to that size for each mating trim piece.

9 To trim the first panel, start with the capping rail that will sit on top, and use a side piece to help position it for a tight-fitting corner (photo K).

10 Remove the side piece while keeping the top piece in place and then nail the top piece to the panel using finish nails (photo L).

11 Repeat for all of the panels, including the tricky ones along the stairs (photo M).

12 Use the miter saw to cut the baseboard, casings, shoe molding, and chair rail, mitering the external corners and using a coping saw to cope the internal ones where necessary (see pages 142-143 for more information about making these cuts).

13 Install the chair rail (photo N), casings, baseboard, and shoe molding using finish nails and either a hammer and nailset or a pneumatic nail gun.

14 Fill any gaps with caulk, and use wood putty to fill any nail holes. Then touch up the panels with fresh paint—and paint the 4-inch spaces between them as well.

15 Reattach the switch and outlet covers and the light fixtures (photo O).

TIPS | DIY Network Home Improvement

REMOVING TRIM

Place a piece of scrap wood behind your flat bar when prying off the trim to protect the walls from damage (photo below).

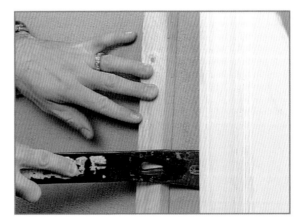

LAYING VINYL STRIP FLOORING

Vinyl laminate flooring is extremely durable and easy to install, and yet it's a dead ringer for a real wood floor. It comes in 3-inch-wide strips that are 3 feet long. These can be cut with shears—no need for a saw—and are simply glued in place—no need for a hammer either.

You Will Need

Screwdriver set	Vinyl laminate flooring strips
Flooring nails	Metal-cutting shears
Hammer	Taping knife
Flat bar	Vinyl laminate adhesive
Putty knife	$\frac{1}{16}$" notched trowel
Rotary sander attached to vacuum	Shoe molding
Rags	Miter saw
Tape measure	Coping saw
Chalk line	Finish nails
Pneumatic nail gun (optional)	

1 Prepare the floor by removing any vent registers and nailing down any loose areas (photo A). Also, remove the shoe-molding using a hammer and flat bar.

2 Next, scrape up debris using a putty knife, and sand the floor lightly with a rotary sander attached to a high filtration vacuum (photo B). Then, wipe the surface with damp rags to pick up any remaining dust.

3 Begin at the room's longest wall, in the doorway if there is one on that wall. Measure 3 inches off the wall at each end and snap a chalk line to help ensure that the first row of strips will be straight. (In this case, the old flooring underneath was perfectly straight, so its seams provided a guideline.)

4 Align the first strip against the door jamb (or the corner, if the wall has no doorway) and mark the cut you'll need on the material (photo C).

5 Use shears to make the cuts (photo D), and then test fit and adjust the cut as necessary. Cut and dry fit the first few pieces of flooring before laying down any glue.

6 Pull up the strips and use a taping knife to put a dollop of vinyl flooring adhesive down (photo E). Use a 1/16-inch notched trowel to spread the adhesive evenly and thinly over the area for the first few rows of flooring against the wall (photo F). Allow the adhesive to dry until it's tacky, which can take up to one hour.

7 Place the first few rows of flooring, starting in the doorway (photo G). Then work one row at a time (photo H), making sure to stagger the seams by 12 to 16 inches for an attractive result and that each piece is pressed tightly against its neighbors. As you go, cut the end pieces using shears.

8 Lay down adhesive for the next few rows, allow it to tack up, and lay down the next batch of flooring strips, one row at a time. It's safe to use the already-laid flooring as a base of operations for the next rows just a few minutes after it's installed (photo I).

9 Install new pre-painted shoe molding by mitering the external corners and using a coping saw to cope the internal ones where necessary (see pages 142-143 for more information about making these cuts). Fasten the pieces with finish nails. Replace the vent registers, and the floor is done.

TIPS | DIY Network
Home Improvement

SAVE THE SCRAPS

When the project is complete, be sure to save some of the scrap wood. It might come in handy later for patching if your new floor gets badly dented or stained.

FOYER FIX-UP

Homeowners Lisa and Rand are avid do-it-your-selfers, but they needed some expert direction when it came to their foyer. The narrow hall felt crowded and dark, so the couple wanted to brighten it up with new flooring and a large picture window looking into the family room. But they had trouble removing the stubborn 1970's floor tile and were unsure about the structural implications of cutting open the wall.

Before: Despite the bright paint colors the homeowners had put on the walls, the narrow foyer felt cramped and dark.

After: A new window over-looking the fami-ly room gives the hallway a feeling of open-ness, as does the new built-in bench where an old coat closet used to be. The new diagonal checkerboard linoleum floor lends cheer and drama to the space.

PROJECT SUMMARY

This job entailed four terrific do-it-yourself projects that any handy homeowner can tackle with the proper steps.

Cutting in a Window. Once it was determined that the wall wasn't load bearing, Karl showed Rand the steps for opening it up and installing a new window.

Laying Linoleum Tile. Amy offered Lisa two different techniques for making fast work of tile demolition. Then the homeowners chose two different tile colors and Amy showed Lisa how to install them in a diagonal checkerboard pattern.

Building a Boot Bench. Turning the old closet at the end of the hall into an open alcove helped to lend a sense of spaciousness to the foyer, and provided space for building a convenient bench where family members can put on shoes before heading outside.

Before: Lisa made slow progress removing the dated ceramic tile floor before Amy showed her how to dispatch it quickly and easily.

CUTTING IN AN INTERIOR WINDOW

To visually open up the dark and claustrophobic foyer, the crew showed the couple how to cut open the wall to the adjoining family room, which is a surprisingly simple job as long as the wall isn't load bearing.

You Will Need

Picture window	3" wood screws
Tape measure and pencil	1½" wood screws
4' level	1' or 2' level
Utility knife	Wood shims
Hammer	Window trim
Reciprocating saw	Miter saw
Flat bar	3" finish nails
Drill/driver	2" finish nails
6" long, ¼" drill bit	Pneumatic nail gun or hammer and nail set
2x4s	Wood putty
Drywall	Acrylic caulk
1¼" drywall screws	

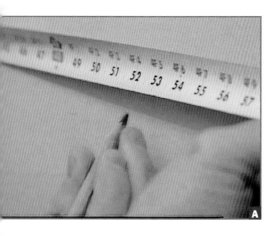

1 Determine the size and location for the window. It's often a good idea to match the height of existing doors or windows, which means creating an opening that's about 2½ inches higher than their jambs to account for framing and trim.

2 Following the rough opening (or "RO") listed on the window packaging, use a tape measure (photo A) and 4-foot level to mark out the opening on the wall with pencil.

3 After double checking those pencil marks for plumb, level, and dimensions, use a utility knife to score the wallboard along the lines (photo B).

4 Use a hammer to punch holes in the drywall across the entire opening (photo C), and look inside the wall to see whether there are any electrical or plumbing lines inside. If there are, hire a professional to relocate them. Many plumbers and electricians offer emergency services, so you're assured of a quick response.

5 Cut the drywall along the scored pencil lines using a reciprocating saw.

6 Remove the drywall by pulling it out with your hands (photo D), using a flat bar to pry it loose if necessary.

7 Use a drill with a long bit to transfer the locations of each corner to the other side by drilling holes through the back of the drywall (photo E). Make sure to hold the drill straight so the hole aligns properly.

8 Move to the opposite side of the wall and use a 4-foot level, to draw straight, level, and plumb pencil lines connecting the four drill holes (photo F).

9 Use a reciprocating saw to cut along the lines, making sure to hold the saw parallel with the floor, and cutting through the wall studs as you go (photo G).

E

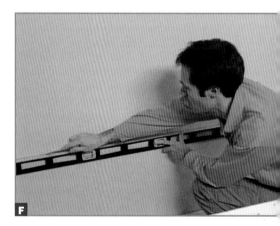

F

G

10 Remove the cut-out in one piece from the exposed-stud side (photo H).

11 Put your tape measure inside the wall just to one side of the opening and drop the tip down as far as it will go. Measure from there to just above the top of the window opening and cut two 2x4s to that size.

12 Insert one of the 2x4s into the wall on either side of the opening, stand it on the bottom plate and align it with the edge of the cut drywall. Use the level to check it for plumb, and then fasten it in place using 1¼-inch drywall screws through the drywall on both sides.

13 Measure the space between the two new 2x4s at the top and bottom of the opening and cut a 2x4 to fit each location. Fasten those in place by screwing through them and into the cut stud ends with 3-inch wood screws (photo I) and by toescrewing (angling) through the ends into the new vertical 2x4s using 1½-inch wood screws.

14 Use the reciprocating saw to trim any excess drywall flush with the face of the new 2x4 frame (photo J). Be careful to keep the blade flat against the face of the wood so you don't cut into it.

TIPS | DIY Network
Home Improvement

LOAD-BEARING WALLS

Never remove any wall framing without first determining whether it's part of a "bearing wall," that is, one that's supporting the building. Making that determination is a job for a contractor, architect, or engineer, who will look at the layout of the walls, the layout of beams in the basement, and the arrangement of rafters in the attic.

15 Use a utility knife to cut a piece of drywall to fit over the new 2x4s around the opening—on each side of the wall—and fasten them using 1¼-inch drywall screws. These won't need taping since they'll be covered with trim.

16 Lift the window into the opening (photo K).

17 Use a 1- or 2-foot level to make sure that the window is flush with the wall surface (photo L).

L

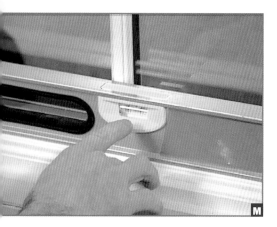

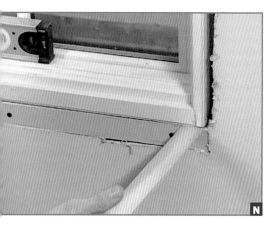

18 Place the level across the bottom of the window to check whether it is level (photo M).

19 Insert wood shims under the corners of the window as necessary to make it level (photo N). To do this, have one person insert the narrow end of a shim from each side so that they overlap. (Don't open the window yet.)

20 Once the window is level, check it for plumb by holding the level against one side. Insert shims between the sides and the jamb as necessary to make it plumb (photo O).

21 Continue to check that the window is flush to the wall as you work, because it can easily slip out of alignment from all of the shimming.

22 Once it's flush, level, and plumb, fasten it in place by sinking 3-inch wood screws through the jamb and shims and into the 2x4 frame that you built (photo P).

23 Use a utility knife to score the shims at the edges of the window jamb (photo Q), and then use your hands to snap them off along that line.

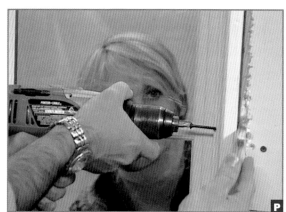

24 Trim out the window using trim that matches the existing trim in your house. For each side, you'll need to measure the top, bottom, left, and right sides of the window from one inner edge of the jamb to the other. Then add ¼ inch to each length.

25 Cut each end of the trim on a miter saw set for 45-degree cuts (or using a miter box and a handsaw). Your window measurement (plus the ¼ inch) should equal the distance between the short ends of the miters (photo R).

26 Fasten the trim to the window by driving 3-inch finish nails into the 2x4 and 2-inch finish nails into the window jamb using a hammer and nail set.Or, to speed things up and reduce the chances of marring the surface, use a pneumatic nail gun (photo S). The extra ¼-inch length allows you to create a "reveal," or setback from the edge of the jamb; put half of the excess on either end of the board (photo T).

27 If the window is operable, remove the clips and straps that hold it shut.

28 Fill the nail holes with wood putty and put a line of acrylic caulk along all edges of the trim. Allow it to dry, and the window is ready for paint.

INSTALLING LINOLEUM TILE

There's a lot to like about linoleum tile for floors. Linoleum is an all-natural, eco-friendly material made from ingredients including jute and linseed oil. It's a traditional material that also comes in an array of contemporary colors and patterns; the tile version is far more DIY-friendly than sheet linoleum. By using tiles, you can create interesting mixes of colors and even install them with a diagonal checkerboard pattern, which is what we're doing here.

A

B

You Will Need

Linoleum tile in two colors	Chalk line
Flat bar	Framing square
Hammer	Heavy-duty tin snips
Vacuum	1/16" notched trowel
Self-leveling concrete	Linoleum adhesive
Taping knife	Rags
Medium-grit sandpaper	100-lb. roller
Pole sander	Shoe molding
Tape measure	

1 Store the linoleum in the room for at least 24 hours before installation so that it can acclimate to the temperature and humidity of the space. Also, if necessary, set the thermostat so that the room is no cooler than 68-degrees from now until the adhesive has dried.

2 Use a flat bar and hammer to remove the shoe molding from the face of the baseboards around the perimeter of the room. You'll install new ones to hide any gaps around the perimeter of the floor once the floor is done.

3 Prepare the subfloor by scraping up any old adhesive and sinking any protruding nail heads. Then vacuum it thoroughly.

4 Mix up a batch of self-leveling concrete following the manufacturer's instructions. This watery, spackle-like product is used to fill holes, seams, and dents, and it's very convenient because it settles into a flat, level surface before it sets up.

5 Use a taping knife to apply a thin layer of the self-leveling concrete to all seams, holes, and dents in the subfloor (photo A).

6 Allow the compound to cure overnight, and then use medium-grit sandpaper loaded into a pole sander to smooth it and the plywood subfloor as well (photo B). Vacuum thoroughly again.

7 Measure each wall and find its center point, then snap a chalk line between opposite center points to create an X in the center of the room, or in this case down the center of the hallway (photo C).

RIPPING UP OLD TILE

The 1970's avocado-colored tile in the foyer had to go, so Lisa began ripping it up with a hammer and a flat screwdriver. Her approach worked, but it was incredibly slow and labor intensive, so Amy showed her a better way—actually, two better ways:

Use a garden spade: This common gardening tool is like a flat, rectangular shovel, and it's an ideal implement to work under the edge of floor tiles in order to pop them loose in bunches.

Rent a hammer drill: Ask the rental company for a matching cold chisel bit instead of the standard drill bits; this powerful machine will make quick work of the job.

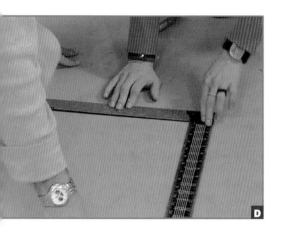

8 Use a framing square to check that the chalk lines form a 90-degree angle, and adjust the lines as necessary until they do (photo D).

9 Lay the first tile over the X, so that each corner meets on a chalk line (photo E). The entire grid will be built off of this tile, so align it perfectly.

10 Weight the tile with a can of adhesive to keep it from moving as you work (photo F)—and also check it often, just to be sure.

11 Set a tile in the other color alongside the first (photo G). Pay attention to the grain of the linoleum, aligning all of the tiles in one color with the grain going one way and all of the tiles in the other color with the grain going the opposite way. Continue laying additional tiles in that quadrant of the floor.

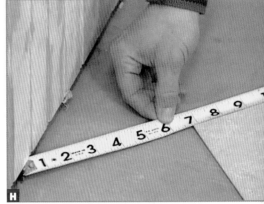

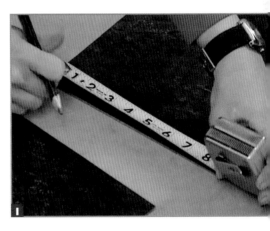

12 Once all of the full tiles are arranged in the quadrant, cut tiles for the edges. Use a tape measure to take the dimensions needed (photo H) at each side of the tile and then to transfer them to the tile (photo I). (Subtract about ¼-inch from each measurement for leeway before you transfer it, since the new shoe molding will cover the edges anyway.)

13 Use a level or framing square as a straight edge and draw a pencil line between the two measurements (photo J).

14 Use large tin snips (heavy-duty scissors intended for cutting sheet metal) to cut the linoleum along the line (photo K).

15 Lay the tile in place (photo L) and repeat for all of the tiles around the perimeter of the space.

16 Once one quadrant of the floor is cut and aligned, pick up all of the tiles, carefully arranging them in piles by row so you can quickly put them back into position without any confusion.

17 Use a taping knife to put a dollop of linoleum adhesive on the floor in the area for the first six or so tiles that you arranged (photo M). Spread it into a thin layer, using a 1/16-inch notched trowel (photo N).

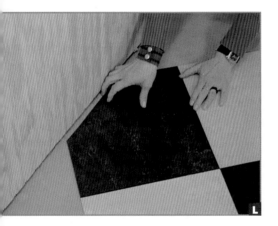

18 Lay the tiles over the adhesive, making sure to align the first one perfectly on the chalk lines and keeping all subsequent ones tight against their neighbors (photo O).

19 Wipe up any adhesive that gets on the tile surface using a damp rag.

20 Before the adhesive dries, use a 100-pound roller to press the completed section firmly in place and to remove any air bubbles (photo P).

21 Move to an adjacent quadrant of the floor, and repeat the process until the floor is done.

22 Once the adhesive is dry, install new shoe molding by coping inner corners and mitering outer corners (see pages 142-143).

A

INSTALLING A BUILT-IN BENCH

To turn a former coat closet into a more welcoming storage alcove, a simple, built-in bench was created. The bench can be added to any foyer, mudroom, alcove, or even doorless closet.

You Will Need

Tape measure and pencil	2" screws
2' level	1x4" board
Electronic stud finder	1½" finish nails
2x4s	¾" birch plywood
Circular saw	Decorative edge trim
Miter saw (optional)	1" finish nails
3" wood screws	

1 Determine the height for your finished bench. For a typical family, about 20 inches is ideal for sitting and removing shoes.

2 Subtract ¾ inch from the finished height that you have selected, measure up from the floor, and make a pencil mark at that height.

3 Transfer that line onto all three walls of the alcove using a level.

4 Use an electronic stud finder to locate the studs, and mark them with a pencil just above the level line.

5 Determine the depth for the bench (a minimum of 16 inches is recommended), subtract 2¼ inches, and cut two 2x4s to that size using a circular saw or miter saw.

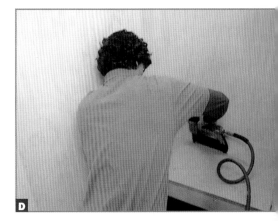

6 Fasten the 2x4s to the side walls by driving 3-inch wood screws through them and into the wall studs.

7 Measure the gap between the two 2x4s along the back wall and cut a 2x4 to that size.

8 Fasten it to the back wall using 3-inch screws sunk into wall studs and toescrewing (angling the screws) it to the side rails with 2-inch screws.

9 Measure the distance between the sidewalls just in front of the two rails, and cut a 2x4 to that size. Install it using 3-inch wood screws sunk into the ends of the side studs.

10 Cut a piece of 1x4 to the same length and attach it to the face of the front 2x4 using 1½-inch finish nails (photo A).

11 Measure the bench from side to side and front to back and use a circular saw to cut a piece of ¾-inch birch plywood to that size (photo B).

12 Lay the plywood over the 2x4s (photo C), and fasten it using 1½-inch finish nails (photo D).

13 Attach a piece of decorative edging over the exposed cut edge of the plywood (photo E) using 1-inch finish nails. Paint as desired when complete.

DIY to the Rescue

7

Garages

If you're looking for ways to add usable square footage to your home, your garage may be an inexpensive alternative to building an addition. Consider the obvious benefits: It's already built, wired, and may even have running water, and chances are there's simply a lot of wasted space. With a little bit of DIY work, your garage can be transformed into a great work space or studio. Alternatively, if your goal is to maximize storage, there are some very simple ways—such as installing a slat-wall mounting system—to increase your usable space and clean up the clutter.

GARDENER'S GARAGE

After retiring from her job as a computer analyst, Gloria could finally devote lots of time to her passion: Gardening. So, she began thinking about creating a garden workshop in her garage—with plenty of efficient tool storage and a large work surface. Unfortunately, the garage was so overflowing with tools and junk that she could barely take one step inside, let alone find whatever it was she had come looking for.

BEFORE: The small garage was packed to the rafters with tools and junk.

AFTER: A good cleanout and an easy-to-install, slat-wall organization system have transformed the space into a well-ordered workshop.

PROJECT SUMMARY

The first—and perhaps most important—step in this job was to clean out the garage. So Amy, Karl, Gloria, and her two sisters all rolled up their sleeves and hauled everything out. Then contractors were brought in to cut out a new doorway to the backyard garden and a large picture window to provide plenty of natural light inside. The team then showed Gloria a simple project that can improve any garage.

Installing a Slat-Wall Organization System. This ingenious product consists of heavy-duty wall paneling designed to mate with dozens of different storage shelves, hooks, brackets, and racks, which can be hung anywhere on the paneled wall. Systems like this are sold by a number of different manufacturers.

INSTALLING A SLAT-WALL ORGANIZATION SYSTEM

Here's a project that can transform the walls of any garage into an orderly tool storage area. All you do is install wall paneling that consists of horizontal slats, and then you can hang a host of hooks, drawers, modular workbenches, tool racks, and shelves anywhere on that paneling. The installation process varies slightly among the different products (so consult the manufacturer's instructions), but it generally works as described here.

You Will Need

Slat-wall paneling and accessories	Framing square
AC finder	Screws
Pencil	Drill/driver
Electronic stud finder	Circular saw
Chalk line	Table saw
4' level	Jigsaw
Tape measure	

After: With an organized workspace and plenty of work surfaces, this once unusable space is now a great gardener's workshop.

1 Use an AC finder (photo A) to determine whether there's any electrical wiring in the walls where you are installing the system. If you find any, mark the locations so that you don't accidentally insert any screws into the wiring. In Gloria's garage, the electrical outlets were surface mounted, so the team removed the screws from the brackets holding them in place, and suspended them out of the way (photo B) to be reattached over the finished slat wall later.

2 Use an electronic stud finder to locate the wall studs at both the top and bottom of the walls, then snap a chalk line between each pair of marks. (In Gloria's garage, this step was unnecessary because the existing nails in the wood paneling identified the stud locations.)

3 Pick a convenient spot on the wall and use a 4-foot level to mark a level line around all of the walls that will be paneled.

4 Measure from the ceiling down to your level line every foot or so to find the lowest point in the ceiling (photo C). Mark that spot with pencil.

5 Measure 12¼ inches down from the low point of the ceiling and make a mark, then use your level to transfer that line onto all of the walls.

6 Place the first piece of slat-wall paneling on top of the level line, and push it all the way to one side of the wall. The product has tongues and grooves, and should be oriented with the groove facing downward (photo D).

7 Fasten the panel in place with screws long enough to sink at least 1½ inches into the studs. Put one screw in every one of the panel's slots at each wall stud (photo E). Pre-drilling is not required, but make sure to set the screw heads flush so they don't interfere with the accessories later.

A new back door provides warm natural light and convenient access to the backyard.

8 Add a panel next to the first and repeat until the first horizontal row is complete, cutting the last piece to size as needed.

9 Begin the second row, making sure that the tongue from the lower panel rides in the groove of the one above and that the joints are staggered by a few feet or more from one row to the next (photo F).

10 Cut the final row to size by ripping the panels along their length. You can use a circular saw, but if you use a table saw you can set the rip fence to the proper dimensions and make quick work of the entire row.

11 Install the corner trim sold by the manufacturer before hanging the panels on an adjacent wall (photo G).

12 Make cuts to accommodate windows, doors, and electrical outlets and switches as you go (photo H) by using a circular saw and jigsaw. Then, assemble and hang the accessories sold by the manufacturer anywhere on the wall (photo I).

ATTIC ACCESS

With five active children in the household, this family's garage had turned into a jumble of outdoor gear, from bikes to bats, sleds to snowboards and holiday decorations to yard tools. As a result, there was no way to park the family minivan in the space—and the mess was a source of endless frustration whenever anyone needed to find anything.

BEFORE: The garage was such a jumbled mess of sports equipment and yard tools that there was no way to park their minivan in the space.

AFTER: Thanks to wall and ceiling storage racks, the Walshes can quickly find whatever gear they're looking for—and they can pile into their minivan on a rainy day without getting wet.

PROJECT SUMMARY

The *DIY to the Rescue* crew installed ceiling- and wall-mounted storage systems, sold at home centers and recreation stores, which you can install following the manufacturers directions.

Installing an Attic Ladder. They also found a major cache of storage space above the garage ceiling and made it accessible by installing a pull-down attic ladder. These prefabricated units are easy to cut into an attic floor and, with a few sheets of plywood providing solid footing above, they'll provide you with a huge storage area you probably never knew you had.

AFTER: A new plywood floor in the crawl space above the garage, and a counterbalanced pull-down ladder that can be operated one-handed, provide plenty of new storage space above the ceiling.

You Will Need

Attic ladder kit	Rip fence	2½" screws
Step ladder	Quick-lock clamps	Wood shims
Hammer	¾" cdx plywood	3" screws
Electronic stud finder and pencil (if no existing attic access panel)	Jigsaw	Utility knife
Chalk line	2" flooring nails, screws, or staples	Drywall and tape (if needed)
Reciprocating saw	Pneumatic stapler (optional)	Trim molding
Tape measure	Pneumatic nail gun (optional)	Miter saw
2-by stock	Drill/driver (optional)	3" finish nails
Circular saw	1x4s	2½" finish nails

INSTALLING AN ATTIC LADDER

If your garage has a flat ceiling and a peaked roof, then there's space in between where you could be storing all sorts of gear. All you need is a pull-down ladder, which looks like a simple trap door but unfurls into sturdy steps that you can quickly climb into the space above. These ladders are counterbalanced with springs, so they're a cinch to operate. If you lay a plywood floor on the joists above, you'll have an easy time moving around in your new storage space as well. (You can also install an attic ladder in the hallway of the main house to add attic access—or to replace a trap door that requires a freestanding ladder.)

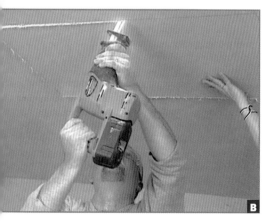

1 Attic ladders are sold as one-piece kits that you simply install in the ceiling for easy access to the storage space above. You'll need to purchase one that's designed for the height of your ceiling. The one being installed here, like most units, is 22½ inches wide, which means that it can be installed between the joists of most garage ceilings. If you purchase a wider ladder—or your joists are only 16 inches apart—you'll need to do some structural framing beyond what is described here. Consult the manufacturer's instructions or a contractor about that.

2 The first step is to climb through the old attic access panel and maneuver yourself up into the space above the floor. From there, pick the exact location of the ladder, arranging it between the joists. Do this by punching nails through the drywall ceiling in the bay between two joists so that the nails are the proper distance apart for the rough opening (or "RO") listed on the ladder's packaging. (If, on the other hand, there is no access panel, use an electronic stud finder to locate the joists so you can choose the ladder location from below.)

3 Snap chalk lines between the nails—or pencil marks if you used a stud finder—to establish the RO that you'll be cutting (photo A).

4 Use a reciprocating saw to cut the drywall or plaster along the chalk lines (photo B). You can start the blade by tapping the back of the saw to force the tip into the drywall—or by starting it flush with the surface and gradually angling it into the ceiling material.

5 Measure the space between the joists at each end of your opening and use a miter saw or circular saw to cut lumber to fit. Use lumber that matches the dimensions of the joists. In this case, they're 2x4s because they're part of a roof truss system.

6 Fasten one of the new boards between the joists at either end of the opening by toe-nailing or toe-screwing, which means angling the fastener through the end of the board and into its neighbor (photo C).

7 If the attic has no floor, lay ¾-inch plywood across the joists before you install the ladder. That's when you can most easily pass the sheets up into the attic through the rough opening.

8 Still, full 4x8 sheets won't fit through the opening, so you'll need to rip them in half. Use quick-lock clamps to temporarily fasten a rip fence to guide your circular saw straight through the plywood. But don't clamp it right down the middle of the plywood. You need to account for the distance between the saw blade and the edge of its bottom plate (photo D), in this case 1½ inches, which put the rip fence at 25½ inches to produce two equal halves.

9 Rip your plywood (photo E) and haul it up into the attic space (photo F).

10 Lay the 2x8 sheets of plywood perpendicular to the joists, making sure that the joints between the boards' ends align at the midpoint of joists. If you have room to work in the space, bring a circular saw up to cut the plywood to length and a jigsaw to make any necessary notches or odd cuts. If you don't have the space to work comfortably and safely, make the cuts down below.

11 Fasten the plywood to the joists using a hammer and 2-inch flooring nails, or a drill/driver and 2-inch drywall screws, or a pneumatic stapler and 2-inch staples (photo G).

12 To install the ladder, first temporarily lay 1x4s across each end of the opening, letting them overlap the opening by about ¼ inch, and fastening them firmly to the framing above using 2½-inch screws (photo H). This will hold the weight of the ladder and keep it flush with the ceiling during the installation.

13 Pass the ladder up through the opening, and then set it onto the temporary braces (photo I). Carefully open the ladder door, without extending the legs (photo J).

14 Place shims between the frame of the ladder and the joists every foot or so around the perimeter of the unit and then sink 3-inch screws through the frame and shims and into the joists (photo K).

15 Remove the temporary 1x4 bracing by backing out the screws.

16 Take off any remaining clips or straps and extend the ladder fully (photo L). Use the provided hardware to attach the ladder extensions (photo M), which allow you to adjust the height slightly to align flush with the floor for sturdy climbing.

17 Score the excess shim material with a utility knife, and then break the shims along those cuts.

18 Close the old ladder access hole—if there was one—by removing the trim, adding 2x4 nailers as necessary,

and patching the hole with drywall and tape following the process described on pages 197-199.

19 Measure the four sides of the opening and use a miter saw to cut trim molding with 45-degree corners to frame the opening. Fasten them to the joists with 3-inch finish nails and to the ladder's frame using 2½-inch finish nails.

8

Outdoor Spaces

The appearance of your home's outdoor areas can be just as important as your indoor spaces. A little concentrated attention to your yard, decks, or doors can have a big payoff: You'll appreciate your outdoor time more, increase the value of your home, and experience a newfound pride in your house every time you return home.

POND PROUD

Katherine and Brian's home didn't need help, but their backyard did. The 1960's concrete pond hadn't been maintained for decades. As a result, it was an overgrown swamp that was filled with green slime and served as a breeding ground for mosquitoes. They wanted to transform it into a healthy fish pond and water garden—sans skeeters—but they didn't know how.

◀ PROJECT SUMMARY ▶

Pulling out all of the overgrown plants and pumping out the fetid water was the easy part. Katherine and Brian's challenge was how to make the pond watertight again, and the process that the *DIY to the Rescue* crew showed them can be used to seal nearly any concrete pond, fountain, or even pool.

Repairing a Concrete Pond. A host of tough aquatic caulks and sealants can repair porous and cracked concrete so that your pond can once again hold water. You just need to know the proper steps to do the job.

BEFORE: The pond was so crowded with overgrown shrubs and weeds that Katherine and Brian didn't even know it was there when they bought the home.

AFTER: With the brush removed; the pond cleaned, sealed and filled with filtered water; and a new Japanese garden planted around it, the "water garden" has become the focal point for the entire backyard. A decorative bridge was built over the pond's waterfall.

You Will Need

Gas-powered sump pump	Rubber gloves
Garden shovel	Rags
Pressure washer	Pond liner primer
Pond caulk	Waterproof tarp
Caulk gun	Neoprene pond sealer
Taping knife	Paintbrushes and rollers
Fast-drying concrete	Plantings and statuary
Concrete trowel	

REPAIRING A CONCRETE POND

Nowadays ponds are often built with fiberglass or rubber liners, but in the 1960s, when the pond was installed, poured concrete was state of the art. Unfortunately, all it takes is a stubborn tree root or years of freezing and thawing to cause cracks and leaks in the old concrete. That's why, in addition to cutting back overgrown plants around the pond and installing a new filter and pump system, the *DIY to the Rescue* team's biggest job was to restore the old concrete shell of the pond.

1 Use a heavy-duty, gasoline-powered sump pump to drain the pond (photo A). (They're available at tool rental stores.) And, shovel out any muck that remains when the water is gone. Rent a pressure washer too, and use it to clean the pond scum from the concrete basin (photo B).

2 Look for cracks, and liberally apply pond-liner caulk to them (photo C), using a taping knife to smooth out the caulk (photo D).

3 If you see any chipped or crumbled concrete, remove it and replace it with a fast-drying concrete, pressing the material into place and then smoothing it out with a concrete trowel.

4 Once the concrete and caulk are dry, don rubber gloves and use rags to apply a coat of pond-liner primer (photo E), which will help the old surface bond to the sealant you'll apply next. Allow it to dry for 45 minutes (or whatever time is recommended on the product packaging).

5 Use paintbrushes and rollers to apply a thick coat of neoprene pond sealant. This creates a rubbery liner over the old concrete. Wait an hour for it to dry, and then apply a second coat (photo F).

6 Add new plantings and statuary around the pond (photo G), and fill it with water using your garden hose.

TIPS | DIY Network Home Improvement

KEEP IT DRY

If there's any threat of rain while the caulk, primer, or sealant are drying, cover the pond with a waterproof tarp to protect it.

Installing a Filter and Pump

The way to keep a pond clean and beautiful—and to prevent it from becoming a mosquito hatchery—is to install a pump and filter system. In the Ambroziak's pond, a pump will draw water out through underground pipes up to the top of an adjacent rock waterfall. Gravity takes care of returning it to the pond. The pump also diverts the water through a biological filter, which uses naturally forming bacteria to remove nitrates and ammonia, as well as a UV sterilizer, which utilizes an ultraviolet light bulb to kill algae. All of this equipment—and instructions for installing it—is available at an aquatics supply store (as well as specialty websites).

CURB APPEAL

Charlie's front entrance was a neighborhood eyesore. In addition to cosmetic problems, such as the peeling paint on the handrail and the serious need for some new yard plantings, the main culprits were an aging slab-plywood front door and a makeshift door surround that had been assembled from leftover aluminum siding.

◀ **PROJECT SUMMARY** ▶

A front entry should be a point of pride, and replacing a rundown door and surround can give a major boost to your home's curb appeal.

Replacing an Entry Door. With a pre-hung door, the door, trim, and jamb are already assembled, and all you have to do is pop them in place.

Installing a Door Surround. You can buy kits in a wide array of styles. Look for a polyurethane product, which won't ever rot or need painting and is so lightweight that only limited fasteners are needed.

BEFORE: A plain-Jane front door and makeshift aluminum siding surround don't do justice to this beautiful early 1900's home.

AFTER: A new six-panel door and classic pediment-and-pilaster surround make for a grand entrance—as do a new stoop surface and railing, which were installed by contractors.

You Will Need

Pre-hung door	Pneumatic nail gun
Flat bar	Nail set
Hammer	Wood shims
Circular saw	Utility knife
Crow bar	Exterior-grade 2- and 3-inch screws
Butyl caulk	Exterior-grade 2-inch finishing nails
Caulking gun	Non-expanding foam insulation spray
4' level	Door knob and lock set

REPLACING AN ENTRY DOOR

The door used for this project is a standard six-panel design, but it's not made from wood. It's a fiberglass product, which offers five times the insulation value of wood. It's also pre-hung, which means that the jamb, trim, and door are already assembled, making the installation job a snap.

1 Remove the hinge pins to get rid of the old door, and then use a flat bar and hammer to remove the door surround, interior and exterior trim, and jambs (photo A).

2 Remove the interior trim from the new door by pulling out the temporary staples.

3 Do a test fit to ensure that the new pre-hung door fits in the opening. Then, remove the door and run two beads of butyl caulk along the subsill (photo B).

4 Slide the door back into place and use a 4-foot level to make it both plumb (perfectly vertical) and level (perfectly horizontal). Fasten the door in place by inserting a few nails through the exterior molding and into the framing (photo C). A pneumatic nail gun greatly reduces the chances of marring the finish with an errant hammer strike.

How to Order a New Door

Whether you're buying a new entry door, an interior door, sliding glass doors, or any other kind of doors, the surest way to get a good fit is to measure the "RO," which stands for rough opening and refers to the space allotted for the door by the structural framing. To do that, remove the interior trim around the door (see step-by-step instructions) and run a measuring tape between the framing members on either side. The opening may not be totally even, so take width measurements at both the top and bottom of the opening and height measurements at both the left and the right. Then, use the smaller of each dimension when ordering your new pre-hung door at the home center.

5 Working from the inside, insert wood shims as necessary between the jamb and framing (photo D) to keep the door level and plumb. On the hinge side, make sure to shim in three locations, including behind each hinge. On the latch side, shim in five locations. Then, sink 3-inch wood screws through the jambs and shims and into the framing.

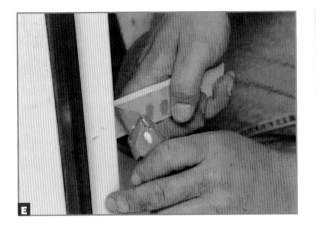

6 Remove the excess shim material by scoring it with a utility knife and then breaking it (photo E).

7 Replace the existing jamb-side hinge screws with 2-inch screws, which will pass through the shims and into the jamb and prevent the door from sagging (photo F).

8 Use non-expanding spray insulation to fill the gaps between the jamb and framing, and then reinstall the interior trim that came with the pre-hung door using 2-inch finish nails (photo G).

9 Attach the door knob and lock sets following the instructions provided with those products.

TIPS | DIY Network
Home Improvement

REMOVING A JAMB
Use a circular saw to slice through the old jamb, and it'll be much easier to pry it out with a crowbar. Just make sure to set the depth gauge on the circular saw properly so that the blade won't cut beyond the jamb.

You Will Need

Polyurethane pediment and pilasters	Drill/driver
Tape measure	Countersink bit
Miter saw	Exterior-grade screws
Construction adhesive	Exterior-grade finishing nails
Caulk gun	Silicone caulk

ENHANCING AN ENTRANCE

To give the door some visual weight, which is more in keeping with the old house than the aluminum surround, the crew installs a pediment and pilasters. These are made from polyurethane, which looks just like wood but doesn't require paint and won't rot.

1 Hold the new pediment in place, center it over the door, and make location marks on the wall just under it at each edge (photo A).

2 Remove the pediment and measure from those marks to the ground to determine the exact size for each pilaster. Transfer those measurements to the pilasters and cut them with a miter saw.

3 Run lines of construction adhesive on the back of one pilaster and put it in place (photo B).

4 Drill a pair of holes on either side of the pilaster at its top, middle, and bottom (photo C). Fasten with screws. For brick walls, use a masonry bit and masonry screws. Repeat the procedure for the other pilaster.

5 Glue up the pediment and position it over the door (photo D), predrilling holes and fastening it with screws as well. Seal all seams with white silicone caulk.

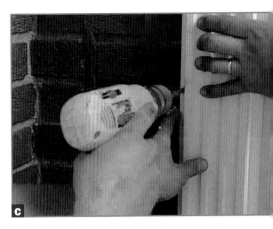

TIPS | DIY Network Home Improvement

USING CONSTRUCTION ADHESIVE

Never apply construction adhesive unless you're ready to install the item immediately, because after a few minutes the glue can form a skin that prevents it from fully adhering to the surface.

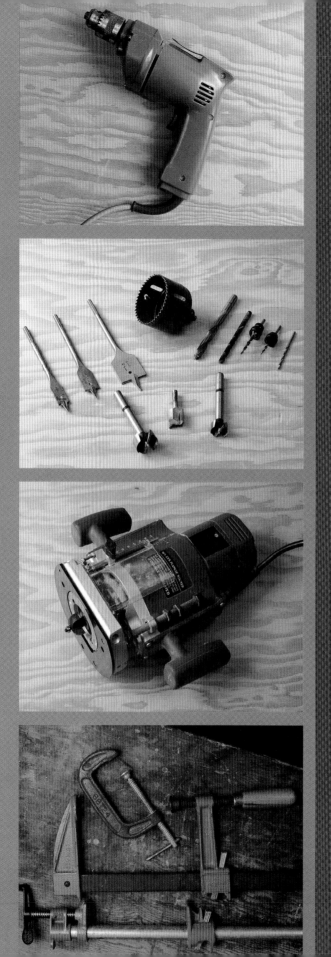

Appendix

In this section you'll find a review of basic tools, materials, and techniques for DIY home projects.

BASIC BUILDING TOOLS

To complete the projects in this book or projects of your own design, you must have the right tools. This section contains an extensive, defined listing of tools for your ideal workshop. Understanding each tool's capabilities is valuable for woodworkers and hobbyists of every experience level. Not all of the tools listed are necessary, but it's a good investment to build a collection of tools needed for most jobs.

An experienced woodworker will recognize that power tools considerably speed up the work process, which will be valuable for a professional. However, a hobbyist should have the freedom to work at his/her own pace and may prefer hand tools. Still, much is to be gained from power tools, which are highly accurate and require less energy to operate than hand tools.

◀ MEASURING AND MARKING TOOLS ▶

The most important step in construction is in the planning, measuring and marking of lengths, joints, and angles. Measuring tools measure length, width and depth. You'll need them at the lumberyard when double-checking stock dimensions, and then back at your workshop when you're building your project. Use your marking tools to designate the lines, points, curves and angles where you must cut or rout.

Steel Tape Measure. Measuring tapes come in lengths of 6' to 25' or more and between ¼" and 1" wide. They are long, bendable rulers which roll up into compact cases. The tape can attach to a work being measured by a hook on one end. It should be loosely mounted to compensate for the width of the hook in measurements. Every ¹⁄₁₆" graduation is noted (and ¹⁄₃₂" increments for the first foot). Our favorite steel tape measure is a ¾" wide, 16' long, self-retracting ruler with a tape-lock button.

Straightedge. When drawing straight lines across short distances, you can't go wrong with a straightedge. A straightedge is basically a steel or aluminum ruler, 12" to 36" long. When graduated clearly, the straightedge can be used for fine measuring and marking.

Combination Square. The combination square is a 4½" x 12" adjustable tool with a sliding blade and a 45-degree built-in shoulder. At any point, the blade can be locked and its end used for measuring and marking.

Try Square. Check or "try" right angles with this square; the ruler along its edges also comes in handy, as do the 6- to 12"-long blades.

Framing Square. Shaped like a large right angle, a framing square is used mainly in construction carpentry to check for 90-degree accuracy on a large scale. Its two edges are 16" x 24" long, and ruler graduations are marked in ⅛" and ¹⁄₁₆" increments.

Scratch Awl. With a scratch awl, you can mark the starting point for a drill bit, or use a sharpened awl to score a line for marking or cutting. The awl is simply a steel point several inches long with a rounded handle. The scribe is a refined version of the scratch awl.

Marking Gauge. Use a marking gauge to scribe a line at a point in relation to an edge. The gauge is a graduated inch-scale beam which can be centered in hardwood stock. A thumbscrew locks the beam in position, and a steel spur at the end marks the wood when the gauge is pushed along the work.

Compass. A compass is used to record and transfer radius arcs, circles, and patterns during the layout process. It has a pivot at the top and two legs, one with a pointed end and one with a pencil tip.

Protractor. A woodworker's protractor simply determines angles. It has a head with a flat base, upon which a pivoting ruler is attached. The ruler is aligned with the angle, which is then indicated in degrees on a graduated scale etched into the head.

Level. A level establishes whether a framing member is level (if it's horizontal) or plumb (if it's vertical). A bubble captured within a small tube of liquid determines the degree off of center the object in question may be. For accurate work, a level of at least 2' in length is needed. The level itself consists of a long, thin frame of aluminum or wood holding three bubble vials, two at the end positioned to read for plumb, and one in the center set to read for level.

◤ PLANING TOOLS ◥

When buying wood, you will find some of it may be rough-cut or surfaced (planed) on one or two sides only. It's up to you to do the rest, to custom-size your own stock, unless you have a woodshop do it for you. Planes are used to bring the thickness of the wood to a uniform level.

Bench Plane. The edge of this hand-held tool's blade, set within a steel frame, is adjusted to protrude slightly from a slot in the sole, or base, of the body. Hand planes are sold in many varieties, but start with a 1¾" to 2" blade and a sole 9" to 10" long.

Other planes, such as the block plane, are used to make the projects in the book. A small hand-sized plane, the block plane has a 2" x 6" body and is used for detail work.

Power Plane. A hand-held power tool used to plane large amounts of stock from a board's surface quickly, a typical power plane has a two-edged rotary blade about 3¼" wide and a sole between 10" and 12" long. A power plane can remove from ¹⁄₃₂" to ¹⁄₁₆" of wood in each pass, depending on its horsepower and the speed of its rotary cutter.

Thickness Planer. A thickness planer is a stationary tool used to plane rough-cut boards to a uniform thickness. Relatively inexpensive, a portable or bench-top planer can handle boards up to 12" wide and 6" thick, removing a maximum of ¹⁄₁₆" of material with each pass. A larger, standing stationary planer costs three to six times more, and can accommodate a board up to 20" wide and 8" thick. Higher-amperage or 220-volt service may be needed for these larger tools.

Jointer. A jointer is a large standing tool designed to level the face of a board and put a consistent and accurate edge on it in preparation for making a joint. A saw blade by itself cannot make a perfectly accurate cut because there's no true reference on a warped board to work from.

Most jointers are stand-mounted and built to handle boards to 6" to 8" wide, though benchtop jointers do exist. In order to cut beveled edges, a large fence was designed to tilt 45 degrees right and left. The truly competitive jointers cut to ½" depth and can complete a ½" rabbet.

◣ CUTTING TOOLS ◢

The number, pitch, bevel, and angle of teeth on its blade determine the function of a saw. The more teeth per inch of blade, or points, the smoother the blade's cut will be. A saw with fewer points will make a coarser cut, but it will also cut more quickly. A backsaw, for instance, with 15 teeth per inch, is adept for fine joinery work; a crosscut saw, given 8 teeth per inch, can tear quickly through thick lumber. Power saws often use combination blades, which cleanly cut both with and against the wood's grain. Various other blades are made to cut other sheet products.

Crosscut Saw. Cut across or against the wood's grain with a crosscut saw. A 26" version will accommodate most of the hand-sawing in this book—with the exception of plywood, though crosscut saw lengths do vary. Crosscut saw teeth vary from 7 to 12 points per inch, depending on how fine of a cut you desire. Remember, the greater the number of points, the smoother and slower the cut will be made.

Ripsaw. Cut with or along the wood's grain with a ripsaw. Most run 26" long and have 4½ to 7 points per inch. If you prefer to use hand tools, you'll need both a ripsaw and crosscut saw because while it is possible to rip with a crosscut saw, you can't make a crosscut with a ripsaw.

Backsaw. A backsaw is a fine-toothed handsaw, and therefore used in joinery to make smooth, accurate cuts. The saw gets its name from the steel back frame fastened to the uppermost edge of the blade.

Table Saw

Backsaws run 4" to 14" in length, and depending on their purpose, they are classified as thumb, gentleman's, and tenon saws.

Coping Saw. A very thin blade, with 10 to 12 teeth per inch, is mounted between the tips of the coping saw's U-shaped steel-bow frame. Cutting curves is a specialty of the coping saw because its frame can be angled away from the line of cut. Typically it cuts boards thinner than ¾".

Miter Box. A miter box is a wooden or metal frame used in conjunction with a backsaw to handcut miters in boards and trim. Beveled miter cuts can be made as well with specially designed compound miter boxes.

Circular Saw. A hand-held, motor-driven saw, the circular saw has a 7¼" blade that's adjustable to angled cuts. The blade penetration varies by degree, from 2¼" at 90 degrees to 1¾" at 45 degrees. Unfortunately, the size and weight of the circular saw negatively affect its accuracy. Be on the lookout for circular saws with carbide-tipped combination blades, though regular, less expensive blades are fine if you clean or replace them regularly. An excellent blade can upgrade the performance of an inexpensive saw.

Compound Miter Saw. A portable power saw that's evolved in several versions, the compound miter saw is also known as a chop saw or cutoff saw. Similar to a circular saw, the least expensive version pulls down to cut and swings from left to right to cut miters. Unlike the circular saw, it's mounted on a short table with a pivoting hinge. A beveling feature that tilts the blade as well for a compound level cut is included in the next level. Our pick is the model with a slide mount so the blade and motor move up and down up to 1' like a radial-arm saw, and it cuts miters and bevels as well. Blade diameters run from 8½" to 12".

Circular Saw

Radial-Arm Saw. Radial-arm saws are stationary power saws used to cross-cut long pieces of wood on a large fixed table. It's a versatile saw with a powerful motor and a 10" blade suspended on a carriage from a beam which can be swung right and left and raised and lowered as well. The saw can also make bevel cuts, and a pivot in the carriage allows the motor and blade to be turned 90 degrees for making rip cuts as well.

Table Saw and Dado Blade. Built into a frame and table, the table saw uses a heavy motor. The table saw's weight and design cuts more accurately than a hand-held circular saw. The blade is raised to a 90-degree cutting depth of 3⅛" (or at 45 degrees, a cutting depth of 2⅛").

A pivoting carriage holds the blade's arbor or axle. Table saws are generally equipped with a 10" carbide-tipped combination blade. Smaller bladed models carry the same features as the larger models. The long, straight bar that runs parallel to the exposed blade and can be adjusted to either side of it is called the rip fence. It ensures that material is being guided to the blade for accurate rip cuts.

A miter gauge helps in making miter cuts. It's adjustable to 45 degrees on either side of its 90-degree midpoint and holds the wood in place at the correct angle as it's being passed through the blade.

Fitted to a table saw, a dado blade is especially designed to make wide grooves and notches. There are two common dado designs: an offset blade that wobbles to the right and to the left as it revolves, and two outer blades and a number of inner "chippers" that are stacked side by side to establish the exact width of the cut.

Jigsaw. A powered alternative to the coping saw, the jigsaw is used for cutting curves, free-form shapes, and large holes in panels or boards up to 1½" thick. It is sometimes called the saber saw. Cutting action is provided by a narrow blade which moves very rapidly. A shoe surrounding the blade can be tilted 45 degrees for angled cuts. The best jigsaws have variable speed control and orbital blade action—meaning the cutting edge is swung forward into the work and back again, through the blade's up-and-down cycle. The jigsaw also comes with a dust blower to keep the cut clear, a circle-cutting guide, and a rip fence.

Utility Knife. This tool can cut thin wood and material, and mark lines for measuring. Look for utility knives with two or three blade positions, including a fully retractable one.

CLAMPING TOOLS

Clamps are quite useful—they hold parts to each other or to the bench so you can mark, drill, or cut them, and they're also great for holding glued parts together while the glue dries. Clamps also function as saw and route guides when used with strips of wood or can be extended to clamp over a large area.

C-Clamps. C-clamps are named after the basic C shape of their steel frames. The anvil end of the C is fixed—it doesn't move at all, while the other end, fit-ted with a threaded rod and swivel panel, is tightened so that whatever it contains is tightly gripped. Use scrap pieces of pads as a buffer so that your work isn't harmed when the clamp is tightened. C-clamps are generally small, though they come in a variety of styles and sizes; woodworking C-clamps are usually limited to a 12" jaw opening, but for the projects in this book, a 4" or 6" size is fine.

Bar and Pipe Clamps. Unlike C-clamps, bar and pipe clamps can hold great expanses of material, like panels or doors, or grip several pieces of wood edged together. Several feet of steel, aluminum, or iron bars or piping make up the clamps. A fixed head, equipped with a short, threaded rod and a metal pad, is at one end, and at the other is a sliding tail stop lockable in any position along the bar or pipe. Pipe clamps are the less expensive option of the two, and they are also more flexible than bar clamps and can be made in excess of 6'. You can purchase pipe clamp kits with the fixtures and be set to go with a bit of help in threading the pipe from your local plumbing supply store.

Vises. A bench-mounted clamp is a vise. It can be used to hold stock securely when you work on it or to hold work pieces together. Better wood vises include a dog—a bar that slides up from the vise's movable jaw to hold work against a similar stop mounted on the bench itself. The dog extends the vise's effective jaw opening by 2' or more. Some vises also use a half-nut to provide quick-slide opening and closing; tightening occurs only once the work is in place. It's important the vise has smooth, broad jaws that are drilled so that facings can be installed to prevent harming fine work.

DRILLING AND BORING TOOLS

Drills and bits are necessary for cutting clean holes through wood. Try drilling functional holes or holes with special features like tapered countersink openings or an open shoulder.

⅜" Variable-Speed Reversible Drill. It's possible to bore any hole with a hand drill, but why waste time and effort when this power drill does the job more quickly and easily. For most any project, a drill with a ⅜" chuck capacity and a motor amperage of 3.5 amps or greater will do just fine. Cordless versions are good for driving screws and drilling small holes, but they may not be suitable for continuous, heavy-duty work.

An electric drill with a variable-speed control is worth the small extra cost. Variable-speed control means the drill's motor is connected to the pressure you exert on the tool's trigger. A reversible motor, included with this model, enables you to take screws out as quickly as you inserted them.

Stop Collars. Stop collars are metal (or sometimes plastic) rings that tighten onto the drill bit's shaft. They are sized to fit different drill-bit diameters and are used to control the depth of a drill bit's penetration. The collar hits the wood's face and stops the bit from going any deeper.

Variable-speed reversible drill

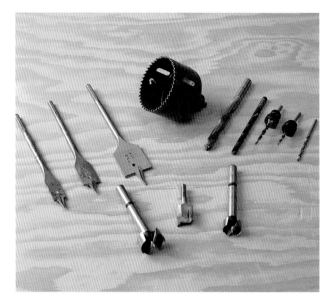

Various specialty bits

Countersinks. There's nothing more unsightly than a protruding screw above the face of wood. Countersinks are used to hide these heads. They fit into the surface of the work by cutting shallow, slope-side holes into which the screw's head rests, flush with the face of the work.

Brace and Bit. A brace is a two-handed drill that operates like a crank—it's most helpful for drilling deep or large-diameter holes cleanly and accurately. At the top of the drill is a handle that allows the crank to pivot and keeps it in line. A two-jawed chuck grips a spiral boring bit, or some type of expansion bit at the lower end. The working hand turns the grip on the crank to slowly bore the opening.

Specialty Bits. There is a variety of drill bits tailored to accomplish specific tasks. For example, use a Forstner bit to drill clean, finely cut flat-bottomed holes. They are made in ¼" to 2¼" diameters. Another bit, the spade bit, is used with power drills to quickly bore and make rough but effective holes through wood. They're designed with a center point and two flat cutting edges and come in ¼" to 1½" diameters.

To bore holes deeper than a normal-length bit would allow, use extension bits or extension shafts over spade bits. The extra-length bits come in diameters from $\frac{3}{16}$" to $\frac{3}{4}$" and usually are 18" long; the spade bit extension shafts come in 18" and 24" lengths and are made to fit standard $\frac{5}{16}$" and $\frac{7}{16}$" power-bit shanks.

To combine the hole-drilling and countersinking processes, use screw bits. Tapered bits, an improvement on the basic screw bits, follow the contour of a standard wood screw; they also include a stop collar. These combination bits are made for screw size Nos. 5 through 12. Versatility is the emphasis of screw bits: not only can you countersink a fastener flush with the wood's surface, but you can also counterbore a deeper hole.

CHISELING AND ROUTING TOOLS

To achieve fine joinery and decorative work, you must have tools able to make sharp, detailed cuts or create a consistent design along the face of a piece of wood. Both power- and hand-operated tools work fine; what matters is the sharpness of the tool's cutting edge.

Chisels. Most projects require the standard mortise chisel. It's a cabinetmaker's tool used to clean up joints and mortises, shave glue and grain from a joint, or simply remove layers of wood from one spot. Try a set of four or five bevel-edge chisels for hand or mallet work, in sizes from $\frac{1}{4}$" to 1" wide.

Routers. A router does many things—it cuts grooves and rabbets, shapes edges and makes slots, all quickly and easily. Rounded or chamfered edges can be cut with a router and a roundover or chamfer bit. You can try to do the same work with gouges, rasps or sanders, but it comes out looking inconsistent.

Router bits are held in a collet on the end of a shaft, which in turn is supported by a flat base and housing. The bit's shape determines what type of cut will be made in the work. Handles on the housing give the operator control of the direction of the bit.

The simplest routers have $\frac{3}{8}$" collets, external clamp-depth controls, and low-amperage motors. More sophisticated models are known as plunge routers; these allow vertical entry into the work for precise cutting and have $\frac{1}{2}$" collets, variable-speed 12- to 15-amp motors, and variable-depth controls.

For best results, use the router on a routing table—a stand with a cast surface that uses a heavy-duty $\frac{1}{2}$" router inverted and mounted from the bottom. An adjustable fence and a special see-through guard allow you to guide the work through the exposed bit safely.

A stationary routing tool, a shaper uses a powerful motor and $\frac{1}{2}$" or $\frac{3}{4}$" spindle to do heavier work than a table-mounted router, such as moldings, heavy raised panels, and hardwood trim.

Router Bits. Note the design and shape of a router bit, as it is reflected in the finished project's edges or grooves. Over 200 router-bit styles are available for various types of work, but for the projects in this book, only a few will be needed. A router bit with a ball-bearing pilot at its tip is used when cutting or shaping an edge—the tip rolls along the edge below the part of the wood being cut, ensuring a high degree of accuracy.

A guide or temporary fence is often used when routing a channel, as groove- or slot-cutting bits cannot use pilot tips. A guide is a device that clamps onto the base of the tool and acts as a moving fence for the router and bit to follow the edge of the work. Set the bit vertically by adjusting the router base to control the depth of cut.

Router

JOINING TOOLS

Now that the boards and components are ready for joining, several tools can be used to complete the joint. You can take the traditional road with back-saws and chisels, or try newer methods.

Doweling Jig. Mainly used for edge-joining and certain framing applications, the doweling jig is a precision frame used to center holes on the edge of a board up to about 2" thick. To correspond with the dowel sizes being used, various-sized holes are on the jig in matching places, so the edges of the joined boards are aligned both vertically and horizontally.

Biscuit Joiners. A high-speed rotary saw with a blade about 4⅛" in diameter and 4 mm thick, the biscuit joiner is also known as the plate joiner. The cutter slices the work horizontally because it is placed on the vertical axis. An adjustable miter fence allows joinery on square and beveled edges. A depth adjuster sets the plunge level to correspond with the size of biscuit being used. Three different sizes of biscuits are available (Nos. 0, 10, and 20), and they range in length from 2⅛" to 2⁹⁄₁₆" and in width from 1⅛" to 1⅞".

HAMMERING AND SETTING TOOLS

Hammers. You'll probably use a lightweight, 3½ to 6 ounce tack hammer to do most finishing work.

Nail set. To set the head of a finishing nail or brad below the surface of the wood without enlarging the hole, a nail set is used.

Mallets. An 8" wooden carpenter's mallet of 12 ounces or so does the work of a larger hammer on chisel work or setting joints. A plastic-headed hammer also works.

Screwdriving Tools. Throughout this book, screw fasteners have a No. 2 Phillips head to give a positive and usually slipless grip. Drive larger Phillips-head screws (No. 12 and up) with a No. 3 Phillips screwdriver tip.

Screwdrivers. A 6" or 8" No. 2 Phillips driver with a molded or wooden handle is the one to use on the No. 6, No. 8 and No. 10 Phillips-head screws usually used in this book's projects. If you choose to use traditional slotted screws, a ³⁄₁₆" and ¼" straight blade are needed. Square-drive screw heads naturally use square-tip drivers.

Power Drivers. To save time, most woodworkers use power-drive bits in combination with cabinet or drywall screws. Often used with hand-held drivers or ⅜" variable-speed power drills, these bits have a short, six-sided shank which slips easily into the drill chuck. Use a tip that's a Phillips or straight-bladed design or a square-drive tip to fit matching screws.

SANDING AND SMOOTHING TOOLS

Before finishing a piece, sanding and smoothing has to be done to level surfaces. Files and rasps cut or round edges and small areas whereas sandpaper prepares the wood for its final finish.

Rasps and Files. Used to make the first cut in removing wood stock for shaping or rounding, wood rasps are coarse-cutting hand tools. A finer cabinet rasp is made for the second round of cutting. Choose from three styles of rasps: flat on both sides, half-round on one side, and round.

Less coarse than rasps, wood files are used for finer smoothing and finishing work. Wood files are about the same size as rasps—10" long, and they usually come in round and half-round cross sections. Only a flat rasp may be needed for this book's projects. It's a good idea to have two grades of files on hand—a 10" or 12" bastard-cut file and a smooth-cut file. The bastard-cut file is one step finer than a coarse file, with a half-round back which allows it to be used on inside curves and arcs. The smooth-cut file, the least coarse of the group, is used for finish work and is especially suited to hardwoods.

Sanders and Sandpaper. Sand by hand or with power sanders. Purchase a hand-sanding block if you choose to sand by hand. The hand-held orbital finishing sander—called a palm or pad sander—has a palm or square pad to which sandpaper is attached. The orbiting mechanism uses a 2-amp motor. The round styles use self-adhesive paper on the pad rather than mechanical clips.

BASIC BUILDING TECHNIQUES

This section is designed for newcomers to woodworking. Beginner builders can get comfortable with the terminology and pick up new techniques by carefully reviewing this section. Experienced woodworkers will find this section worthy of review, too—it's a chance to refresh your memory of basic skills and terminology.

MEASURING AND MARKING

The preliminary measuring and marking stage is as important as buying the right tools. It's all about how you use the tools: you shouldn't rely on a tape measure to make a straight line or a square blade to make a circle. It's also important to stick with the same tools throughout the completion of the project—switching tapes or marking gauges in midstream is the cause of many small mistakes.

Most general measuring begins with the steel tape because it's fast and accurate within $\frac{1}{16}$"—acceptable for almost any but the finest of woodworking projects. A steel tape has its limitations, though. For example, it can't mark a straight line over any distance: the metal band will move or distort no matter how careful you are. For distances less than 3', rely on a straightedge for marking a straight line.

For a greater distance, try a chalk line—a chalking string stretched between two points—or you can use the steel tape to mark short increments over a greater distance, then strike lines between them with a straightedge if need be.

For marking for a cut, most woodworkers use a steel scribe or a pointed awl trip. However, a sharp pencil can be used to make a very accurate V-shaped mark, pointing to the cutting site.

Use a square to mark a square, perpendicular edge, crosscuts, or transfer a line to the remaining three sides of a board. For smaller jobs, use a try square, and for larger projects, use a framing square. Lay the stock, or handle, of the tool against the edge of the work and mark a line, in pencil, along the blade. For transferring the line to the side and back surfaces, walk the square around the work, using the tail of the previous line as the start of the next one, and so on.

Use a compass for laying out a radius of partial or full circles. Open its legs to the correct radius, then place the point at the center of the circle or arc you wish to make and swing the other leg to make the mark. A radius is half a circle's width, or diameter. A protractor simplifies measuring angles. Either the

Measuring and marking tools

CUTTING STRAIGHTS AND CURVES

After the measuring and marking, making the cuts is a matter of following the lines. Remember to double-check your work: measure twice, cut once.

To rip, saw with the grain of the wood. Grip handsaws firmly, but not tensely, with the back of the handle squarely against the ball of your palm. Use the outer edge of your thumb to guide the teeth when starting a cut. The cut should be made on the waste, or outer side, of the line. Begin the cut on the upstroke; the sides of the blade must be squared with the surface of the wood.

For crosscuts, hold tools at a 45-degree angle; with rip cuts, work at 60 degrees. Deliver the cutting pressure only on the downstroke.

When using a circular saw, make sure the teeth fully penetrate the opposite face of the work by setting the blade depth—adjust it by loosening a knob and moving the shoe up or down. This will clear sawdust particles and make the blades less likely to jam. Also, be careful not to cut your sawhorse or workbench.

Carefully set yourself in a comfortable position before using the saw, but remember not to lean too far forward, otherwise you'll end up off balance at the end of a long cut. Be careful not to grip the handle too tightly either—it'll tire your hands and possibly create inaccuracies in your work. Some larger saws come with a second grip; however, remember that clamping is required with two-handed saws.

Remember to always wear safety glasses when using any saw. Watch the power cord; be sure to draw it behind you before starting the tool. Sight your line of cut along the reference mark on the front of the saw's shoe. The safety guard swings up by itself as you progress with the saw.

A table saw cuts more accurately than a circular saw thanks to its guide fence and miter gauge. A handwheel located at the front of the saw cabinet sets the cutting depth; judge the depth of cut by watching the blade—several full teeth should be exposed during the cut, which cools the blade and allows sawdust to escape.

standard transparent protractor or the stainless steel kind with degree-graduations along the edge is fine. Match the bottom of the protractor with the work's baseline. Read the measurement at the top arc. A more sophisticated bevel protractor has a pivoting arm that makes it easier to read or establish the existing angle or bevel.

Establish the degree off of "plumb" (straight up-and-down) or "level" (horizontally straight) of a framing member with a level. Lay the level's frame against the side or top of the framing member. Watch the bubble in the appropriate vial—for plumb measurement, use the end vials; use the center vial for determining level—to see how true the piece is. Remember, a centered bubble is perfectly accurate.

Loosen the lock and slide the fence to the right or left as needed to adjust the fence. To measure the width of the cut, use the gauge on the fence rails, or for greater accuracy, take a steel-tape reading between the fence's edge and the tip of a blade tooth set toward the fence.

Once you start the motor, give it a few seconds to come up to speed; never shove a piece of wood into a slowly moving blade. Don't ever put your hands near the spinning blade; use a push stick about 18" in length to pass the work through.

The basic curve-cutting tool for thinner material and very taut contours is a thin-bladed coping saw because it's easily controlled. For stock more than ⅜" thick, or a line greater than the throat depth of the saw, use a handheld electric jigsaw. Tighter curves or circles require thinner jigsaw blades so that the jigsaw doesn't bind or overheat.

There are several ways to cut at an angle, just as there are several ways to make miters and bevels. Miters are angle-cuts made across the face of a board, for example, the corners of a picture frame; bevels are angle cuts into the edge of a board, as in a piece of trim or molding. Finally, a compound cut is a combination of miters and beveling. For wood less than 6" wide, use a miter box with a fine backsaw for the most accurate miter cut.

For bevel cutting, adjust the shoe on a circular saw to a 45-degree angle. For even greater accuracy, adjust the table saw blade to the same angle by using the handwheel on the side of the cabinet.

For mitering with a table saw, loosen the knob on the miter gauge and adjust its fence to the desired angle, then tighten the knob. Hold the work against the fence, so that the gauge and the work move forward to meet the blade.

Cut a rabbet or groove with a table saw fitted with a dado blade, or use a router and straight bit. Remember that when using the table saw you must remove the table insert and dado blade width.

There are two ways to do this, depending on the blade design. The width of an offset "wobbler" blade is changed by a rotating hub, while a stacked type must be set out of the saw and reinstalled on the arbor. Make sure that the teeth rest between the gullets of the adjacent blades and that the chippers are staggered around the circumference when you stack the chippers between the outer blades.

The handwheel adjusts the depth of the blade and sets the fence to establish the position of the rabbet or groove on the work. Be careful not to cut too quickly as the blade has a lot to do cutting that much wood at once.

GROOVING AND JOINING

Clean and straightened surfaces that haven't been fully cut with a saw or drill are required for mortises and mortised hinges. This is accomplished with a chisel, which is fairly easy to do as long as the chisel has a consistently sharp edge.

A mallet isn't necessary for most work; push the work by holding the chisel in your right hand while using your left hand to guide the blade's direction. Mallet users should strike the tool lightly to avoid taking big bites at once. Hold the tool at a slight right or left angle whenever possible while working with the grain to ensure smooth cuts that are less likely to dull the blade. Avoid gouging the work by not driving the edge too steeply—hold the blade at a slight downward angle.

A router handles deeper cuts or shaping work quickly and cleanly, while it would take quite some time with a saw and chisel. The finished edge or groove's look is determined by the shape of the router bit's cutting surface. A slot the width of the bit itself is made by a straight bit; a clean, rounded edge is cut into a squared surface by a roundover bit; a beveled edge is cut by a chamfer bit; a detailed profile is cut by an ogee.

Position yourself with two hands loosely gripping the router and a clear view of the working bit when operating a router, and be sure to wear safety goggles. Movement is from left to right, except when circular or irregular cutting, in which case the motion is counter-clockwise. First make cuts across the end grain of your work, then avoid chipping by working with the grain.

Control the depth of cut by loosening the base of the router and adjusting the motor housing up or down. To preview what your work will look like, run a test on a piece of scrap wood before you make any permanent cuts. Your control of the tool will improve with practice, and soon you'll be able to rely on the depth gauge marked on the side of the router rather than having to test every cut you make.

Freehand work is fine for short jobs; however, when making long cuts, you'll need to clamp the wood to a bench and use the tool's base-mounted guide to keep the cut straight. If without a guide, substitute by clamping a straight section of 1 x 2 to the bench or your work parallel to the line you wish to cut.

Place a piece of scrap stock to the right and left of the work, flush with the working surface, to rout narrow stock or edge–rabbet grooves—this prevents the routing guide from tilting to one side and spoiling the cut and gives you a place to mount a guide if you use one.

DRILLING AND COUNTERSINKING

Three parts make up the screw hole: the pilot or lead hole (which is little more than half the diameter of the screw itself), the shank or body hole (the same diameter as the screw), and the sink or bore, used if the screw head is to be recessed below the surface of the wood.

You only need to drill the pilot hole for a short screw in softwoods, though dense hardwoods and long screws sometimes call for a shank hole, too. Remember, make that hole only as deep as the shank—the unthreaded portion of the screw—is long. Also remember that a screw driven perpendicular to the grain has twice the holding power than a screw driven to the wood's end-grain.

Screw bits (countersink and pilot bits) considerably simplify the hole-drilling process. Sized by screw numbers, screw bits have top collars and counter-sinks adjustable for length. Tapered bits are used to accommodate wood screws perfectly.

When driving into softwoods using 1½" or shorter No. 6 and No. 8 diameters, cabinet screws are even easier to use. These self-tapping, power-driven screws don't need pilot holes, though you should take care to predrill the pilots when working near the end of the wood.

Deck screws, another variation, are coated with a smooth anodization which makes them weather-resistant. They work in both softwoods and hard-woods, though in hardwoods, the screw holes should be predrilled, otherwise you may split the wood or shear the screw head off.

A regular bit can drill socket holes if the diameters are small enough—¼" or ⅜". For larger holes, you'll need a Forstner bit, which produces a clean, flat-bottomed hole. If you have trouble gauging the depth of a socket correctly, use a stop collar or piece of tape on a standard drill bit.

If another piece is planned to face it, take care when drilling through-holes. In this situation, you can avoid splintering wood by drilling only partially through the piece, then coming at the hole from the opposite side. To locate the point at which you'll start the second hole, use a small pilot bit to penetrate the back face.

CLAMPING

Clamps hold parts together while they're being glued or secure pieces for cutting or drilling. Long and relatively inexpensive for their size, bar or pipe clamps are especially suited for wide clamping jobs. A range of adjustment between the jaws is permitted by a sliding tailpiece.

For joints or pieces less than 12" in depth, choose a C-clamp. Available in standard and deep throat depth, C-clamps all have a threaded rod with a swivel tip that applies pressure to the work as you tighten the rod. Cut 2" square pads from scrap pieces of ¼" plywood to prevent the metal tips from marring your work.

Place the clamp's pressure points directly at the centerline of the work or joint to be glued for the best results in joint-clamping. Be careful to snug-tighten, not over-tighten, as over-tightening can damage the wood, and with gluing, squeeze enough adhesive from the joint to cause uneven distribution and a weakened bond.

◢ SANDING AND SMOOTHING ◣

Finishing really depends on the quality of the wood, as well as your technique. With a lot of time and a bit of know-how, you'll perfectly sand or smooth the wood's surface.

Before you get started, take a look at the surface in good light. Before you can safely apply a coating, the wood must be flat with a smooth surface. Check for glue runs or forced material, which should be cleared off before they dry. Otherwise, trim the dried material off with a sharp chisel.

Beware of manufactured wood pieces, especially moldings and trim, which may be contaminated with silicone oils or waxes left there as cutter-head lubricants. Don't fret, they can be removed with a cloth soaked in mineral spirits, followed by an ammonia wash of one part clear ammonia to 15 parts warm water spread evenly over the entire surface then wiped dry. It also depends on the type of your finish: waxes and oils are usually fine with oil-based finishes, but can ruin water-based finishes and lacquers,

Clamps

Power sander

which is why they must be removed before going any further.

It's time for a quick lesson on sandpaper, or more accurately: coated abrasive. Sandpaper is made of tiny pieces of mineral grit glued onto some kind of backing. Determining how fast a paper will sand, grit also reflects how much effort will be required to sand. Both the backing and the glue, or binder, used to keep the grit in place determine how the grit will stand up to wear and solvents.

Sandpapering is a straightforward process: the abrasive removes tool marks left in the surface of the wood and replaces them with grooves established by the size of the grit on the sandpaper. The errant large grooves are replaced with the sandpaper's many small grooves, especially if a fine grit is used.

"Open coat" and "closed coat" are terms used to describe the amount of grit on the backing. With only 50 percent to 70 percent of the surface covered in mineral, open coat paper provides a place for the cuttings to lodge, and occasionally requires declogging. Completely covered with sand, a closed coat offers a finer finish. Higher-grit (extra-fine) papers don't offer much more because most of the grooves have already been sanded off. To conserve material and make less heat, however, stick with the lower-numbered grits (open style paper).

Grits are made of either synthetic or natural material. Many different materials are available, but only a few apply to wordworking. Of the synthetic grits, you'll probably use aluminum oxide. Light brown or white in color, it's ideal for general sanding and finishing work. If using only one product to finish, use another synthetic, silicon carbide, which is bright black.

Even with the popularity of synthetics, garnet, a reddish mineral, is used often in sandpaper. Breaking off as it works, garnet presents a new sharp facet with each fracture. Though garnet works wonderfully, it does wear faster than synthetics.

Sandpaper backing varies according to the tool it is used with. Both sheet and polyester cloth backings are used, though cloth backings are used more commonly on belt sanders. Hand-held palm sanders commonly have a paper backing with pressure-sensitive adhesive.

Always work from coarse to fine grits when sanding. Begin with an 80 or 100 grit, then progressively increase the point range with each step. A typical progression would be 80/120/220/400.

Choosing grit size is critical. Too heavy a grit usually results in a lot of work with little progress because you're simply creating grooves, while too light a grit doesn't remove the deeper marks created earlier, leaving them in the finish. With softwoods, you usually don't have to sand finer than 180 grit. However, the harder woods may require a 400-grit or higher. Generally speaking, we recommend a 220-grit sanding for the best results, particularly with a water-based finish.

An alternative to the motor-driven palm sander, a sanding block achieves a flat surface while giving you a better feel for your work. Fold a paper sheet several times to do detail work, or stiffen the paper in your fingers. At the 150-grit level or higher, you may sand in any direction because the scratches will likely be invisible.

When using a palm sander, the most common error is scrubbing it across the wood's surface too quickly. Remember that an oscillating sander already moves at the rate of nearly 14,000 oscillations per minute—you don't need to speed it up. To

Palm sander

give you an idea of the ideal speed, your hand (with the sander in it) should move about one inch per second—this should prevent swirl marks from ending up in the finish.

Metric Conversion Table

Inches	Decimal Inches	Rounded Metric	Inches	Decimal Inches	Rounded Metric	Inches	Decimal Inches	Rounded Metric
1/16	.0625	1.6 mm/.16 cm	7½	7.5	19 cm	18		45.7 cm
1/8	.0125	3 mm/.3 cm	7¾	7.75	19.7 cm	18¼	18.25	46.4 cm
3/16	.1875	5 mm/.5 cm	8		20.3 cm	18½	18.5	47 cm
¼	.25	6 mm/.6 cm	8¼	8.25	21 cm	18¾	18.75	47.6 cm
5/16	.3125	8 mm/.8 cm	8½	8.5	21.6 cm	19		48.3 cm
3/8	.375	9.5 mm/.95 cm	8¾	8.75	22.2 cm	19¼	19.25	48.9 cm
7/16	.4375	1.1 cm	9		22.9 cm	19½	19.5	49.5 cm
½	.5	1.3 cm	9¼	9.25	23.5 cm	19¾	19.75	50.2 cm
9/16	.5625	1.4 cm	9½	9.5	24.1 cm	20		50.8 cm
5/8	.625	1.6 cm	9¾	9.75	24.8 cm	20¼	20.25	51.4 cm
11/16	.6875	1.7 cm	10		25.4 cm	20½	20.5	52.1 cm
¾	.75	1.9 cm	10¼	10.25	26 cm	20¾	20.75	52.7 cm
13/16	.8125	2.1 cm	10½	10.5	26.7 cm	21		53.3 cm
7/8	.875	2.2 cm	10¾	10.75	27.3 cm	21¼	21.25	54 cm
15/16	.9375	2.4 cm	11		27.9 cm	21½	21.5	54.6 cm
			11¼	11.25	28.6 cm	21¾	21.75	55.2 cm
1		2.5 cm	11½	11.5	29.2 cm	22		55.9 cm
1¼	1.25	3.2 cm	11¾	11.75	30 cm	22¼	22.25	56.5 cm
1½	1.5	3.8 cm	12		30.5 cm	22½	22.5	57.2 cm
1¾	1.75	4.4 cm	12¼	12.25	31.1 cm	22¾	22.75	57.8 cm
2		5 cm	12½	12.5	31.8 cm	23		58.4 cm
2¼	2.25	5.7 cm	12¾	12.75	32.4 cm	23¼	23.25	59 cm
2½	2.5	6.4 cm	13		33 cm	23½	23.5	59.7 cm
2¾	2.75	7 cm	13¼	13.25	33.7 cm	23¾	23.75	60.3 cm
3		7.6 cm	13½	13.5	34.3 cm	24		61 cm
3¼	3.25	8.3 cm	13¾	13.75	35 cm	24¼	24.25	61.6 cm
3½	3.5	8.9 cm	14		35.6 cm	24½	24.5	62.2 cm
3¾	3.75	9.5 cm	14¼	14.25	36.2 cm	24¾	24.75	62.9 cm
4		10.2 cm	14½	14.5	36.8 cm	25		63.5 cm
4¼	4.25	10.8 cm	14¾	14.75	37.5 cm	25¼	25.25	64.1 cm
4½	4.5	11.4 cm	15		38.1 cm	25½	25.5	64.8 cm
4¾	4.75	12 cm	15¼	15.25	38.7 cm	25¾	25.75	65.4 cm
5		12.7 cm	15½	15.5	39.4 cm	26		66 cm
5¼	5.25	13.3 cm	15¾	15.75	40 cm	26¼	26.25	66.7 cm
5½	5.5	14 cm	16		40.6 cm	26½	26.5	67.3 cm
5¾	5.75	14.6 cm	16¼	16.25	41.3 cm	26¾	26.75	68 cm
6		15.2 cm	16½	16.5	41.9 cm	27		68.6 cm
6¼	6.25	15.9 cm	16¾	16.75	42.5 cm	27¼	27.25	69.2 cm
6½	6.5	16.5 cm	17		43.2 cm	27½	27.5	69.9 cm
6¾	6.75	17.1 cm	17¼	17.25	43.8 cm	27¾	27.75	70.5 cm
7		17.8 cm	17½	17.5	44.5 cm	28		71.1 cm
7¼	7.25	18.4 cm	17¾	17.75	45.1 cm			

INDEX